WITHDRAWN FROM
COLLECTION

CHRONIC PAIN
AN INVISIBLE ILLNESS

By Kelly Gurnett

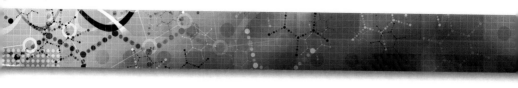

Published in 2018 by
Lucent Press, an Imprint of Greenhaven Publishing, LLC
353 3rd Avenue
Suite 255
New York, NY 10010

Designer: Deanna Paternostro
Editor: Jennifer Lombardo

Cataloging-in-Publication Data

Names: Gurnett, Kelly.
Title: Chronic pain: an invisible illness / Kelly Gurnett.
Description: New York : Lucent Press, 2018. | Series: Diseases and disorders | Includes index.
Identifiers: ISBN 9781534562844 (pbk.) | ISBN 9781534561960 (library bound) | ISBN 9781534561953 (ebook)
Subjects: LCSH: Chronic diseases in children–Juvenile literature. | Chronic diseases–Juvenile literature. | Chronically ill–Juvenile literature.
Classification: LCC RJ380.G87 2018 | DDC 618.92′044–dc23

Printed in the United States of America

CPSIA compliance information: Batch #CW18KL: For further information contact Greenhaven Publishing LLC, New York, New York at 1-844-317-7404.

Please visit our website, www.greenhavenpublishing.com. For a free color catalog of all our high-quality books, call toll free 1-844-317-7404 or fax 1-844-317-7405.

CONTENTS

Illness is an unfortunate part of life, and it is one that is often misunderstood. Thanks to advances in science and technology, people have been aware for many years that diseases such as the flu, pneumonia, and chicken pox are caused by viruses and bacteria. These diseases all cause physical symptoms that people can see and understand, and many people have dealt with these diseases themselves. However, sometimes diseases that were previously unknown in most of the world turn into epidemics and spread across the globe. Without an awareness of the method by which these diseases are spread—through the air, through human waste or fluids, through sexual contact, or by some other method—people cannot take the proper precautions to prevent further contamination. Panic often accompanies epidemics as a result of this lack of knowledge.

Knowledge is power in the case of mental disorders, as well. Mental disorders are just as common as physical disorders, but due to a lack of awareness among the general public, they are often stigmatized. Scientists have studied them for years and have found that they are generally caused by hormonal imbalances in the brain, but they have not yet determined with certainty what causes those imbalances or how to fix them. Because even mild mental illness is stigmatized in Western society, many people prefer not to talk about it.

Chronic pain disorders are also not well understood—even by researchers—and do not yet have foolproof treatments. People who have a mental disorder or a disease or disorder that causes them to feel chronic pain can be the target of uninformed opinions. People who do not have these disorders sometimes struggle to understand how difficult it can be to deal with the symptoms. These disorders are often termed "invisible illnesses" because no one can see the symptoms; this leads many people to doubt that they exist or are serious problems. Additionally, people who have an undiagnosed disorder may understand that they are experiencing the world in a different way than their peers, but they have no one to turn to for answers.

Misinformation about all kinds of ailments is often spread through personal anecdotes, social media, and even news sources. This series aims to present accurate information about both physical and mental conditions so young adults will have a better understanding of them. Each volume discusses the symptoms of a particular disease or disorder, ways it is currently being treated, and the research that is being done to understand it further. Advice for people who may be suffering from a disorder is included, as well as information for their loved ones about how best to support them.

With fully cited quotes, a list of recommended books and websites for further research, and informational charts, this series provides young adults with a factual introduction to common illnesses. By learning more about these ailments, they will be better able to prevent the spread of contagious diseases, show compassion to people who are dealing with invisible illnesses, and take charge of their own health.

WHAT MAKES CHRONIC PAIN DIFFERENT?

Pain is a part of life everyone experiences. It comes in many forms, from the sharp sting of a cut to the throbbing of a stubbed toe. Normally, pain serves an important purpose. It is the body's way of warning that something is wrong. It can signal danger, such as the pain of accidentally touching a hot stove, or warn of illness, such as the sore throat that starts off a cold. Pain can also occur as the result of injury and prevent further injury to a body part that is already hurt. For example, a twisted ankle is painful to put weight on, which encourages shifting weight to the other leg, allowing the injury to heal without the risk of further damage.

When a person's body is functioning normally, pain works as an alarm bell that warns of a harmful condition that requires attention. However, for millions of people, pain is more than just a symptom of a temporary condition; it is a constant problem that affects every part of their daily lives. It may occur as a result of an injury or illness, or it may occur by itself as the result of a glitch in one or more systems

Normally, pain is the body's way of signaling something is wrong.

of the body. When pain persists for a long period of time and does not go away or get better, it goes from being a symptom of another condition to its own condition. This condition is known as chronic pain syndrome.

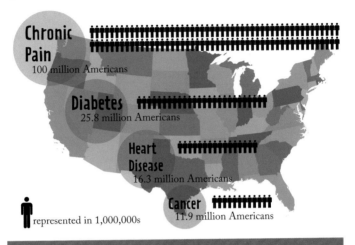

Chronic Pain
100 million Americans

Diabetes
25.8 million Americans

Heart Disease
16.3 million Americans

Cancer
11.9 million Americans

represented in 1,000,000s

Nearly twice as many people in the United States suffer from chronic pain as from diabetes, heart disease, and cancer combined, as this information from MedLanding shows.

In a 2011 report called *Relieving Pain in America: A Blueprint for Transforming Prevention, Care, Education, and Research*, the Institute of Medicine (IOM) found that approximately 100 million Americans suffered from chronic pain. Of those people, 25 percent suffered from moderate to severe pain, while 10 percent suffered from "severe disabling chronic pain."[1] The Mayo Clinic lists chronic pain as "a leading cause of disability in the United States and one of the most common medical problems people face."[2] However, it is still largely misunderstood. One poll found that "only 18 percent of respondents said they believe that chronic pain is a major health problem."[3] While great advances have been made in the way the world approaches chronic pain, there is still much to be done.

CHAPTER ONE

UNDERSTANDING CHRONIC PAIN

The truth is that as advanced as modern medicine may be in treating acute (short-term) pain, there is still no "cure" for chronic (long-term) pain. However, research continues, and the next big medical advance could be on the horizon. The first step in helping those with chronic pain is to understand how pain works—both in general and in those with chronic conditions.

Not the Same as Normal Pain

The pain most people are familiar with is acute pain. Acute pain generally has a clear cause that can be identified, such as an injury or illness. When someone has acute pain, it is easy for them to tell a doctor exactly where the pain is coming from. As a result, acute pain is fairly easy to treat. It lasts for a relatively short time—anywhere from a few days to a few months. Sometimes a simple over-the-counter medication helps decrease acute pain, and sometimes prescription medication or other treatment is needed. Once the original cause of the pain has been taken care of, the pain eventually goes away.

Acute pain may affect someone's life for a period of time, causing them to miss out on some of their normal activities, but they know an end is in sight. They are also likely to receive support from friends and family; people send "get well" cards, bring over

Acute pain is made easier by an eventual recovery and the support of loved ones.

food, or offer to help with daily tasks. If the pain is not too strong, they may even be able to "power through" and continue going to work, attending school, or hanging out with friends.

Chronic pain, on the other hand, lasts at least three to six months, but it often lasts longer and is typically much harder to understand than acute pain. Some chronic pain sufferers can pinpoint the start of their pain to a particular injury or illness, such as a car accident that caused damage to the spine. However, once their body heals, the pain is still present, even though for most people it would have gone away. Other chronic pain sufferers experience pain because a system in their body is not working right, such as nerves that do not send signals properly. As chronic pain sufferer Melanie Thernstrom wrote in her book *The Pain Chronicles*, "Acute pain is like a well-functioning alarm signaling danger; it ends when the fire does. Chronic pain ... is like a broken alarm that rings continuously, signalling only its own brokenness."[4]

Unlike acute pain, the majority of chronic pain conditions have no cure and never truly go away. Patients can learn to manage their symptoms, and they may have days when they are nearly pain-free. However, unlike temporary acute pain, chronic pain is a lifelong condition that can seriously interfere with a person's ability to live a normal life.

While acute pain can cause a person to miss out on some activities, chronic pain may cause them to lose their job, their friendships, and their ability to

Chronic pain can have a negative effect on a sufferer's mental health.

enjoy their favorite things. It can affect their mental health as well as their physical health. Additionally, one of the most frustrating aspects is that it can be hard for chronic pain sufferers to make the people in their lives understand what they are going through because chronic pain is mostly invisible. As pain writer and scholar David B. Morris put it, "Chronic pain and acute pain are as different as cancer and the common cold."[5]

Understanding and Treating Pain Throughout History

Early civilizations such as the ancient Greeks and ancient Babylonians believed the gods used pain to punish the wicked. As a result, pain was seen as a sign of the presence of evil in the patient's mind or soul. Since pain was thought to be of a divine nature, these civilizations turned to priests for healing in the form of sacred rituals; potions; and procedures such as trepanation, in which holes were drilled into a patient's skull in the hopes of releasing evil spirits.

Early Christians believed pain had a divine origin as well. In the Biblical story of the Garden of Eden, God punishes Eve for eating the forbidden fruit by banishing her from paradise and sentencing women to feel pain during childbirth. Jews and Christians also saw pain as a tool used by God to test their faith. In the story of Job, Job is forced to endure horrible pain and suffering so he can prove that he will believe in God no matter what. Since pain was thought to have a holy purpose, people were encouraged to accept it and learn to live with it. Some believers even caused pain to themselves or willingly accepted pain at the hands of others as a way to demonstrate their love for God and become closer to God.

With the Enlightenment of the 18th century came a better understanding of the human body and how disease works. Scientists and doctors began to see the connection between people's habits and living conditions and the spread of disease; this led to public health programs designed to stop disease by increasing the overall standard of living. Scientists in the 19th and 20th centuries discovered that pain had a biological origin—namely, nerve endings that send pain messages to the brain. They learned pain was a signal that warned of disease and injury, and therefore the way to end pain was to treat the disease or injury that was causing it. For the first time, pain was viewed not as something that was meant to be lived with but as something that could be fixed. The invention of anesthetics such as ether and medications such as opioids—those based on the opium poppy—added to a new sense of optimism around pain relief.

In recent decades, scientists and doctors have begun to understand the way other factors influence pain. Pain is not simply a physical

Modern medicine allows doctors to identify the source of many forms of acute pain.

symptom as a result of physical causes; it can also be affected by a person's emotional state, environment, relationships and more. Similarly, it affects all parts of a person's life, not just how they feel physically. As a result, treatments such as counseling, alternative medicine, and support groups have risen in popularity.

The Downside of Pain Relief Advances

While scientific and medical advances have brought hope and relief to many people with acute pain, they can also make things harder for those living with chronic pain. The more powerful science becomes in healing acute pain, the harder it is for people to understand why it cannot fix chronic pain. When anesthesia was first used in the 1840s to make surgery less painful, *The People's Journal* of London published a piece that boldly exclaimed, "WE HAVE CONQUERED PAIN."[6] The fact that some pain cannot be conquered continues to confuse and frustrate doctors and patients alike.

"Healthy people don't understand how a person can be sick for months and years and have doctors still not know what's wrong with her," said Aviva Brandt, who lives with chronic pain, fatigue, and infections, among other issues. "Some people get a funny look in their eye, like they think it must all be in my head because otherwise wouldn't I have a diagnosis by now? Medical science is so advanced, with all this technology and such, so how come good doctors can't figure out what's wrong with me?"[7]

It can be hard for people to understand why doctors cannot "fix" chronic pain.

Current Attitudes with an Outdated Origin

Today, there is a better understanding of what causes pain. However, some mistaken attitudes toward pain are still very common and can be traced back to the way pain was viewed in the past. Below are some mistaken beliefs about pain that are influenced by the way pain used to be understood.

Current Attitude	Old Belief
What have I done to deserve this?	Pain is punishment for evil.
Suck it up, and move on.	Pain is a test that must be suffered through.
I don't want to complain.	Living with pain is a virtue. If you cannot handle pain, you must be weak.
Have you tried [treatment/ drug/doctor]?	Science can fix everything. If you are sick, it must be because you have not found the right cure.
I don't want people to know I'm sick because they might judge me.	If you are in pain, it must be because you have done something wrong in the past or you are doing something wrong now.
It's all in your head.	If science cannot cure your pain, you must be making it up or exaggerating it.

What Causes Pain?

When the body works the way it should, there are two main reasons why pain occurs: illness or injury. In these cases, pain serves as a warning that triggers the body to start the healing process. This kind of pain is generally acute and disappears once the injury or illness has been taken care of.

Sometimes injury or illness creates lasting damage to the body. Nerves may send pain messages at the wrong times. The pain pathway may be damaged, causing the body to misunderstand pain messages and send out warnings when nothing is actually the matter. Although the original injury or illness may have healed, the person continues to feel pain long afterward. There are also medical conditions that can cause chronic pain on their own.

How the Body Processes Pain

People feel pain as a result of messages that are sent through the body on a pathway known as the nervous system. The nervous system is made up of two parts: the central nervous system, which includes the brain and spinal cord, and the peripheral nervous system, which branches out from the spinal cord to the internal organs, muscles, joints, and skin.

Peripheral nerves have special nerve endings called nociceptors that can sense when something unpleasant or harmful is happening to part of the body. Different nociceptors sense different kinds of pain; there are nociceptors that sense pressure, temperature changes, tissue damage, and more. When one of these nerve endings senses pain, it sends a message to the spinal cord or brain. These messages travel at different speeds depending on how serious the pain is. Mild or moderate pain such as a stomachache travels on slower pathways, while severe pain such as a broken bone travels on faster pathways.

When the pain message gets to the spinal cord, it is processed by nerve cells that work as gatekeepers, determining whether or not the message should continue on to the brain. Extreme pain and pain related to danger, such as the burn of touching a hot stove, are allowed through the "gate" quickly so the body can respond to it right away. Less urgent pain, such as a minor scratch, may not be allowed through at all. This is why people may sometimes find small cuts

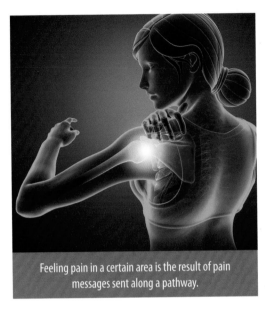

Feeling pain in a certain area is the result of pain messages sent along a pathway.

or bruises on their body that they do not remember getting.

It is only when a pain message reaches the brain that the person actually begins to become aware of it and start feeling it. This whole process takes a split second. The brain then analyzes and sorts the pain message so the body can take the appropriate actions. It may cause emotions such as fear or anxiety that make the person more aware of danger as well as causing the body to take a physical action, such as pulling a hand back from a hot stove. It also causes the body to respond to the illness or injury, such as sending more blood and nutrients to an area that was hurt so it can begin to heal. Additionally, the brain releases natural painkillers called endorphins and sends "stop pain" signals to control pain and let the body know when an injury or illness has been responded to.

The Role of Thoughts and Emotions

When it comes to how strongly a person feels pain, it is important to note the difference between pain threshold and pain tolerance. Pain threshold is the point at which something causes a person to feel pain. It varies based on factors such as family history, biological sex, and life events. Pain tolerance is how much pain a person can stand. It depends on how someone thinks and feels about their pain. Pain tolerance can be affected by multiple factors, including how much

Other Factors That Influence Pain

Different factors can influence whether a person develops chronic pain over the course of their lifetime. The IOM breaks these factors up into four "life cycle" categories, and they include:

Birth and Early Years

- genetics, or the traits inherited from parents
- biological sex (women are at greater risk of developing chronic pain)
- race (people of color are at greater risk)
- prematurity (when a baby is born before its due date)
- feeding and sleeping schedules
- parents' personalities and attitudes

Childhood

- abuse, trauma, or recurring painful experiences
- poverty
- serious illness or injury, or hospitalization
- emotional problems
- being separated from the mother

Adolescence (Preteen and Teenage Years)

- puberty and hormone changes
- injury
- obesity
- lack of physical fitness

Adulthood

- lack of social support (friends, close family, etc.)
- accumulated or chronic stress
- surgery
- wear and tear on joints and muscles
- job-related unhappiness
- aging

sleep a person has gotten recently, their past experiences of pain, and how much control they believe they have over their pain.

Negative emotions such as resentment and anger can make pain feel more intense, while positive emotions such as acceptance and humor can lessen pain's intensity. A small child may scream when they get their first shot at the doctor's office because they are not used to the experience and are scared. As the child gets older and learns that shots are not a big deal, they may be able to handle the pinch of a shot without fussing. Not knowing what is causing pain can make a person feel that pain more strongly, while getting an official diagnosis that explains their symptoms can help them deal with the pain. "Pain catastrophizing"—constantly worrying and obsessing over pain—can make that pain feel even worse.

Negative emotions such as worry and fear can make pain feel stronger.

One study found that soldiers who had surgery for injuries received in battle needed less pain medication than civilians who had the same surgery. Researchers believed this was because the soldiers saw surgery as "a minor matter compared with what they had experienced in battle."[8] Similarly, an athlete who has spent years training and playing through pain may be able to compete with an injury that would stop most people in their tracks because the athlete has learned to ignore it. In other words, "attitude affects your pain, for better or worse."[9]

Neuroplasticity: When Pain Causes Pain

The central nervous system does not just process

pain messages; it can also be rewired by pain messages due to something known as neuroplasticity. This is when the brain changes as it takes in new information. Neuroplasticity is generally a good thing; it allows a person to gain new skills such as playing an instrument or learning their way around a new city. However, for someone with chronic pain, neuroplasticity can actually be harmful.

The longer the nervous system processes pain messages, the better the pain pathways get at sending these messages. Pain messages move faster, the body becomes more sensitive to pain, and sometimes pain messages are created when there is nothing to cause them. At the same time, nerves can also be damaged, preventing them from sending the "stop pain" signals they would normally send. These changes explain why chronic pain often gets worse over time, even when there is no additional damage to nerves or tissue. In these cases, pain actually causes the body to train itself to feel more pain.

Neuroplasticity also explains why some chronic pain patients develop pain from harmless stimuli, known as allodynia. This occurs when nerves that normally sense harmless sensations become extra-sensitive and start to send pain messages for even light touches. As a result, "a caress can feel like a blow, and the light pressure of a sock can feel like … hot iron shoes … Patients become, literally, afraid to move."[10] In another condition, known as hyperalgesia, pain messages get more intense, causing the pain to feel much worse than it normally would. There are many different conditions that can cause chronic pain, and sometimes the source of the pain plays a role in how intense it is.

CHAPTER TWO

CHRONIC PAIN CONDITIONS

With chronic pain conditions, people's bodies do not work the way they should. For them, pain is not a symptom of illness or injury; it is a disorder all by itself that cannot be "cured" the way acute pain can. Although there are many conditions that can cause chronic pain, some are more common and well-known than others.

Headaches

Headaches are one of the most common forms of chronic pain. For most people, headaches are infrequent and go away after time, but chronic headache sufferers deal with headaches on a regular basis.

The most common type of headache is a tension headache. Tension headaches generally occur when the muscles in the skull tighten. This can be due to stressful things such as getting into a fight with a friend or getting stuck in a traffic jam. Spending a lot

Everyone gets headaches, but sometimes they become chronic.

of time in front of a computer screen can also cause a tension headache. Tension headaches can be mild or severe. They feel like pressure is being put on the forehead, sides of the head, scalp, or back of the neck. Sometimes there is also a throbbing or burning feeling. Everyday tension headaches eventually go away after rest or with over-the-counter medication, but for some people, they become a chronic problem.

Migraines are headaches so extreme they can put a person's life on hold, and more than 20 million Americans experience them. Symptoms include a severe throbbing pain on one side of the head, sensitivity to light and sound, and nausea or vomiting. Scientists are unsure exactly what causes them, but they have some theories. One is that they are caused when the chemicals in the brain are not balanced due to things such as hormone swings or certain foods. In the past, it was believed that these chemical imbalances affected blood flow in the brain, but many researchers now believe certain people are more likely to experience migraines due to genetics, or traits passed down from parent to child. Research is still ongoing, but whatever the reason, it is undeniable that many people experience severe pain from this condition. Migraines can last anywhere from a few hours to three days.

Cluster headaches are not very common, but they are even more intense than migraines. The pain has been described as feeling "like a hot poker being stabbed into your eye or a drill bit boring into your skull."[11] Other symptoms include pain on one side of the head; red, watery eyes; runny nose; and a drooping eyelid. These headaches can happen over several days or weeks, often at the same time each day, and they generally last between 30 and 90 minutes, although they can be as short as 15 minutes or as long as 3 hours. They are called cluster headaches because they occur in a cluster, or small group. A person who gets them will experience between one and three headaches per day. Months may go by between each cluster of headaches. Medical experts are still unsure what causes cluster headaches, but they seem to be affected by changes in season as well as heavy smoking and drinking. Men are more likely than women to experience cluster headaches.

Back Pain

Back pain is another very common form of chronic pain. It can be caused by an injury or accident, such as a car crash, a fall, or trying to lift a heavy object. For most people, back pain heals in a month or so, but for some it can become a lifelong condition.

Back pain does not always go away.

Some people experience a form of back pain known as sciatica. The sciatic nerve runs down each leg. If it becomes pinched or irritated, it causes symptoms such as numbness, tingling, and muscle weakness. Other people experience back pain when one of the discs in the back bulges or bursts. This can happen as a result of injury or normal wear and tear, and it is known as a herniated disc, sometimes nicknamed a "slipped disc." Discs are special pieces of tissue that act as shock absorbers between the bones in the spine. When ones of these discs is herniated, it places pressure on nearby nerves, causing pain.

Arthritis

Arthritis causes pain and stiffness in the joints, which are the places where bones meet; they allow the body to bend and move. At first, arthritis sufferers may only feel mild pain when they use their joints. However, over time, the pain can get worse and may even occur when they are not using the inflamed joints at all.

There are two common types of arthritis. Osteoarthritis occurs when the cartilage—the flexible tissue that cushions the bones in the joints—wears down. This caus-

Arthritis affects joints in places such as the fingers and wrists.

es the bones to rub up against each other, creating inflammation. The body's attempts to fix this damage can cause bony lumps, or spurs, to form in the joints, especially those in the hands and feet. Osteoarthritis is often caused by years of wear and tear on the joints; as a result, people who are 45 or older are more likely to have it.

Rheumatoid arthritis occurs when the immune system, which normally fights off disease, attacks the lining of the joints instead. This causes inflammation—redness, swelling, and heat—in the joints, which leads to swelling. This swelling prompts the body to produce chemicals that can damage the joints. Joints begin to lose their shape and may even be destroyed altogether. In addition to inflammation, rheumatoid arthritis sufferers may also experience stiffness in their joints and muscles and difficulty moving. This form of arthritis generally occurs in people 30 to 50 years old, and it affects nearly twice as many women as men.

Myalgic Encephalomyelitis/Chronic Fatigue Syndrome (ME/CFS)

ME/CFS causes extreme, long-lasting fatigue, or tiredness, as well as joint and muscle pain, sore throat, headaches, and trouble with concentration and memory. Symptoms may get worse with physical or mental activity, and sleeping or resting does little to relieve the sense of total exhaustion. Symptoms may develop over time or start suddenly. The cause of ME/CFS is not yet known, although some scientists believe it may be connected to an infection, immune system issue, or hormone imbalance. ME/CFS affects more women than men.

Chronic fatigue is more than just feeling tired; getting extra sleep rarely helps.

Fibromyalgia

Fibromyalgia is a disorder that causes pain in the tissues around the joints. Symptoms include aching all over, stiffness, numbness, tingling, feeling tired all the time, difficulty sleeping, digestive problems, and sensitivity to temperature. Fibromyalgia symptoms do not follow a particular pattern. They come and go, and they can also be different from patient to patient. As a result, doctors often diagnose a person with fibromyalgia only when they have ruled out a number of other possible reasons for the symptoms. Most patients are diagnosed during middle age. The cause of fibromyalgia is still unknown.

Other Common Conditions

Irritable bowel syndrome (IBS) is a disorder that causes a wide range of digestive problems. Symptoms include stomach pain, bloating and gas, constipation, and diarrhea. While the cause of IBS is unknown, it is likely its symptoms are made worse by stress, activity level, and diet.

Stomach pain is one symptom of IBS.

Temporomandibular joint disorders (TMDs) affect the hinged joints that connect the jawbone to the skull, allowing the mouth to open and close. Symptoms include pain in the face, neck, and ears; jaw locking, which occurs when a person is unable to open or close their mouth; a popping or clicking sound in the jaw; and headaches. TMD's cause is not known for certain, but it may be a result of the joints wearing down, damage to the joints, or problems with the jaw muscles.

Endometriosis is a condition that affects women, generally starting after they get their first period. It occurs when the lining of the uterus drifts out of the uterus and implants itself in other pelvic organs.

One symptom of endometriosis is severe cramping.

Symptoms include pain in the lower parts of the body, severe cramping during periods, pain when going to the bathroom, and pain during sex. Endometriosis may negatively affect a woman's ability to get pregnant. Pain medications may help, but generally the only real treatment is surgery to remove the extra uterine tissue. However, if it is left untreated for too long, even surgery may not completely eliminate the pain.

Lesser-Known Conditions

In addition to the above conditions, there are many lesser-known conditions that can cause chronic pain. Like those described above, the same patient can have more than one of these conditions. They include:

- mitochondrial myopathy, in which the cells of the body do not produce enough energy

- myofascial pain syndrome, in which trigger points on the body cause pain in unrelated parts of the body

- complex regional pain syndrome (CRPS), in which pain from an injury or surgery—generally in the limbs—lasts longer and is stronger than it should be

- Ehlers-Danlos Syndrome, in which the body's connective tissues are too flexible and fragile

Getting a Diagnosis

It can be hard for chronic pain sufferers to get a diagnosis because their symptoms are often hard to pin down; "there are no universal, definitive tests for pain,"[12] and many conditions have symptoms that can be confused for other conditions. Finding a diagnosis is often a process of elimination.

Some conditions can be diagnosed by certain tests, such as mitochondrial myopathy, which can be diagnosed by analyzing muscle biopsy samples. However, sometimes patients are simply labeled as having "chronic pain"—a broad label that results in hit-or-miss treatment plans that fail to consider the patient's specific symptoms, health history, and needs.

Getting a diagnosis may seem like a scary thing, but many chronic pain sufferers feel better emotionally when they finally find out what is wrong, especially since they may have been told previously that the problem was all in their head. "I first heard the word 'endometriosis' in college after I had already been to several other doctors, been prescribed Tylenol 3 for my pain, and been on birth control since I was 15," Cait Telaak said. "It was a minor relief to finally have a diagnosis."[13]

CHAPTER THREE

THE EFFECTS OF CHRONIC PAIN

Living with chronic pain can affect all aspects of a person's life, including their mood, their relationships, their career, and more. As Dr. Lynn R. Webster, who specialized in pain treatment, wrote, "Pain … affects the whole person."[14]

Physical Effects

When a person is in constant pain, they can find it hard to do things most people take for granted. Hanging out with friends, doing chores, and even taking a shower can be difficult and exhausting. As chronic pain patient Kristen Spinola wrote on the website The Mighty, "Most chronic pain patients fight like crazy to live a normal life."[15] An invitation to see a movie is much more complicated for them, she said, because

> in their head they have considered if they can sit still that long, how much medication it would require, if they have the energy, if they will stay awake through the movie, how high their pain is now and how it might increase, if they go will it make getting through tomorrow harder, and most importantly, given all this, will it be any fun.[16]

Feeling pain in one area of the body can also cause a person to do certain things that make another part of the body hurt. Adjusting one's posture to deal with arthritis pain can cause new pain in the lower back. Clenching one's jaw or tightening one's neck or shoulders because of a migraine causes new pain in these areas.

Being in chronic pain makes people less interested in being physically active. However, staying active is an important part of staying healthy. Not getting enough physical activity can lead to weight gain, weakened muscles and bones, increased body fat, a weakened immune system, and conditions such as heart disease and diabetes. These things, in turn, can cause even more negative symptoms, creating a vicious cycle.

It can also be hard to sleep with chronic pain. From falling asleep to staying asleep, pain can interfere with getting a good night's rest, which in turn, can lead to sleepiness and low energy the next day. A Gallup poll sponsored by the National Sleep Foundation found that "62 percent of people with chronic pain reported waking too early because of their pain and being unable to fall back asleep."[17]

Emotional Effects

Pain is more than just a physical experience; "a pain condition affects everything a person is, and everything a person is affects her pain."[18] Feelings of frustration, anger, sadness, and loneliness are common among chronic pain sufferers as they face the daily struggle of living with their symptoms as well as the knowledge that the pain will never completely go away. "It's hard to not have control over your everyday routines—to not be able to just go and do something without a ton of planning ahead of time," said Melissa McLaughlin, who lives with CFS and fibromyalgia.

It's hard to live in ... what I've always called the "untils" ... until something else goes wrong, until something improves, until there's a new drug that actually works for you, until there's an upswing in your symptoms ... It's hard to see your peers doing things with their lives that you want to be doing

Living with chronic pain can make someone feel lonely, sad, and frustrated.

with yours, and to know that you're just not physically capable of doing those things right now—or might never be.[19]

Fear and worry are also a natural reaction to chronic pain. "When I'm faced with a beautiful day and I'm contemplating a walk, my head is calculating its very own spreadsheet of costs versus benefits," Spinola wrote.

Will enjoying 15 minutes of walking in the sun mean I'm [in pain] for the next day? Three days? Five days? A week? How high is my pain now? Will this help or hinder? How high is my stress? Will this help or hinder? How is my mood? How is my fatigue? ... What do I need to do over the next few days? Will I be able to do it? ... At best I can guess and more often than not, I'm very, very wrong. "Don't you want to go for a walk on a nice sunny day?" seems like a very simple question, but to someone suffering from chronic illness and pain, we left simple behind a long time ago.[20]

As many as half of chronic pain patients develop mood disorders such as anxiety and depression. According to Dr. Michael Clark, director of Johns Hopkins Hospital's pain treatment program, as many as "one-third to three-quarters of people with chronic pain experience moderate to severe depression."[21] It is estimated that as many as 50 percent of chronic pain sufferers consider suicide at some point.

Negative emotions of any kind can make pain feel stronger, and dismissing those negative thoughts is a separate battle; it is not always easy to think positively, and this can make people irritable. However, it is not fair to either the person with chronic pain or their loved ones to dismiss hurtful words and actions by blaming the illness. It makes friends and family feel upset and guilty, and it creates a sense of powerlessness for the person with the disorder. Feeling constantly out of control of their actions can increase the negative emotions chronic pain sufferers feel as a result of their illness, but knowing that they do have control over how they react to their illness can give them a sense of empowerment.

Many people feel that responsibility is the same thing as blame, but this is not true. People with any kind of chronic pain disorder are not to blame for their feelings, but if their words or actions are hurtful to others, they should try to make amends. For instance, if someone's pain is making them feel irritable and they say something harsh to a loved one, they should apologize when they feel calmer. They should not tell the person, "I don't owe you an apology because my pain makes me irritable and therefore I can't be held accountable for anything I say."

Cognitive Effects

Chronic pain can cause the brain to decline and break down. Dr. A. Vania Apkarian of Northwestern University did a study of the effect of chronic pain on the gray matter of patients' brains, which is what helps with processing information and memory. The study found that chronic pain

> *dramatically reduced the gray matter of the patients' brains ... While normal aging causes gray*

The Emotional Cycle of Pain

Living with chronic pain can be an emotional roller-coaster ride, made up of the following five stages, according to the Mayo Clinic:

Stage 1: Fear/Concern

The person worries about what is causing their pain. Focusing on their pain makes it feel worse, which makes them worry more.

Stage 2: Hope

Getting a diagnosis is a relief and eases the person's fear. Given the power of modern medicine, they are hopeful their doctor will be able to make them feel better.

Stage 3: Anger/Depression

When the pain does not get better, even after many different doctors and treatments, they become angry, frustrated, and hopeless. They may take these feelings out on other people or turn to bad habits as a way to ease their suffering.

Stage 4: Guilt/Withdrawal

They feel bad for being angry with others and guilty because they have to depend on others to help them with things. To avoid this, they stop going out as often or telling people how they are really feeling.

Stage 5: Renewed Hope, Followed by Depression

Over time, the person learns to accept their new "normal." New treatments and lifestyle changes help them start feeling better. Excited, they push themselves and wind up feeling bad all over again. Eventually, the pain drives them to find a new treatment, which starts the cycle over again.

matter to [decrease] by half a percent a year, the gray matter of chronic pain patients [decreases] dramatically faster: the pain patients showed losses amounting to between 5 and 11 percent, the equivalent of ten to twenty years of aging.[22]

As a result, pain patients may experience cognitive symptoms such as difficulty concentrating, thinking, and remembering things. Together, these effects are sometimes called "brain fog."

"It feels like I'm trying to concentrate on things with dogs barking in my ears," said Ryan Gurnett, who suffers from mitochondrial myopathy, among other conditions. "No thought is safe for more than

20 seconds. I can try to hold onto the thoughts in my head, but they're fleeting. It sometimes feels like I'm losing my mind, and it's scary."[23]

Quality of Life Decrease

Quality of life is "a concept that considers not only the medical measures of your condition—whether you give your pain a 3 or a 7, for example, or how far you can bend your knee—but emotional, social, and other subject aspects of life as well."[24] Since pain affects all parts of a person's life, it can have a serious impact on their overall quality of life.

Chronic pain can change a person's relationships with friends, family, and others. While people may be supportive at first, after some time, they may grow tired of hearing about a person's pain, understanding when the person cancels plans, or helping out with things the person can no longer do. Christy Kassler, who suffers from mitochondrial myopathy, lives with her parents and relies on them for things such as meals and help getting in and out of the bathtub when her pain gets especially bad. While she appreciates their support, she also believes that "they definitely resent how much I need them to do because they want to have lives of their own. They'd rather go out than stay in with a sick, depressing daughter all the time."[25]

Because it is hard to see chronic pain the way it is possible to see something such as a broken leg, people have trouble understanding how sick someone with chronic pain really is. They may look fine, which leads

Loved ones may make an extra effort to help someone in chronic pain, but over time, their relationships may be affected.

some people to suspect they are making up their symptoms or exaggerating how bad they really are. This can lead to frustration, anger, and resentment, eventually ending some relationships. According to Telaak,

> *I have lost friends and have a hard time connecting with new people because of my pain. I feel like a flake for having to ask for schedule changes because I don't feel well, and I am reluctant to open up to new people and have to explain my condition all over again. The pain makes me feel isolated. In many ways, chronic pain sufferers face a lonely path.*[26]

Chronic pain conditions also "have a direct impact on a patient's ability to maintain various roles and identities."[27] When a person can no longer work or do the hobbies that bring them joy and satisfaction, they can feel a real sense of loss. "I have worked with people who had full, rich lives as corporate leaders, mothers, athletes and professors before their chronic pain," said Rachel Noble Benner, a mental health counselor and researcher at Johns Hopkins University. "However, by the time I saw them, they were isolated, overmedicated and depressed, and they believed their life was devoid of meaning."[28]

Chronic pain can also force a person to reconsider the goals they had for their life. "I am somewhat fortunate in being able to predict when my pain will be the worst, so I try to schedule light around that time," Telaak said. "It makes me reluctant to become a parent; I often wonder how I could be an effective mom if I'm out of commission for a full week each month."[29]

Getting Used to a New "Normal"

People with chronic pain have to learn to let go of the life they used to lead and adjust to a new reality. Their old goals and expectations are often no longer reasonable, given their physical limitations. This affects all aspects of their life—from relationships to career to hobbies—and it can be hard to accept. Adjusting to a new "normal" has been described as being similar to the grieving process, which includes five stages: denial, anger, depression, bargaining, and finally acceptance.

Chronic pain sufferer Crystal Fudalik described how difficult her adjustment period was:

> *When fibromyalgia and arthritis hit me hard a few years ago, it was a huge change. I went from being driven to do well in school, and later the work world, to finding I couldn't work at all. With no children, few friends, and a society that sees your career as a major part of your identity, the loss of self was just as hard as dealing with the many symptoms of my illness.*[30]

Everyday errands such as grocery shopping can be much harder with chronic pain.

Chronic pain sufferers can find it hard to keep a job for a number of reasons. Pain and exhaustion can prevent them from concentrating or performing at their highest levels. Even when they have good days, it can be difficult to predict when these days will occur, and most jobs have strict attendance policies that are hard to stick to with unpredictable symptoms. Some chronic pain sufferers are unable to work at all, which can lead to additional problems such as a sense of guilt and frustration. Lauren Brooke, who suffers

Pain Cycle Syndrome

People with chronic pain can fall into what is called a "vicious cycle" of pain if they do not manage their energy carefully. This cycle includes the following stages:

Stage 1: Decrease in Activity

Pain makes it hard to do daily tasks such as cleaning the house, so the person puts these things off, hoping they will feel better the next day.

Stage 2: Increase in Activity

When they do feel better, they push themselves too hard. There is so much to get done and they do not know how they will feel the next day, so they do everything they can while they are feeling up to it.

Stage 3: More Pain, Less Activity

Overdoing it makes them feel awful the next day. They are forced to rest, sometimes for days. Eventually, they stop trying to do things altogether to avoid more pain.

Stage 4: Loss of Strength and Physical Conditioning

Some physical activity is necessary to keep the body strong, so not doing enough actually makes their pain worse. It also makes it much harder when they do try to do something.

Stage 5: Withdrawal and Isolation

They stay home more and more, and their friends and family stop inviting them out. They get lonely, and being by themselves makes them focus more on their pain. The next time they have a good day, they are ready to make the most of it and do as much as they can—which only starts the cycle over again.

The more pain sufferers stay isolated, the lonelier they get and the more they focus on their pain.

from arthritis, wrote on The Mighty,

> *[W]hat was so painful was that I was being judged because I didn't work, not for who I was as a person. It didn't matter that [I] was [a] good person and what my morals and values were. No, all that mattered was that I didn't work.*

> *What's so ironic about it is that I feel I work very hard. As a matter of fact, I work a full-time job 365 days a year. It's a job called managing my chronic pain. It's merciless, unforgiving and unrewarding. It's not a job I chose and not something I get paid for.*[31]

Those who are able to work face their own challenges. Bosses and coworkers may not understand the frequent sick days a chronic pain sufferer is forced to take or the way their symptoms can affect their workload. Too much stress can make symptoms worse, which can prompt some people to cut back their hours, take a part-time job rather than a full-time job, or take a job with less stress that does not pay nearly as much.

Telaak explained some of the interpersonal problems people with chronic pain deal with at work:

> *I sometimes consider more advanced positions in my career field, but this is another area where it's*

Pain can make it hard for people to concentrate or do their best at work.

scary to have to navigate my situation with a new boss. I also don't want days where I'm not spot-on to affect my team, and I take that into consideration with job opportunities as well.[32]

Health Care Issues

With medication costs, visits to doctors and specialists, and other treatments, chronic pain sufferers face a larger amount of medical costs than the average person. However, many health care plans are not designed to help with these extra costs. "Many of those who are receiving medical care for pain are dissatisfied with their treatment and continue to endure moderate to severe pain," Webster said. "Not getting proper treatment now, however, can lead to even more medical costs down the road."[33]

Webster went on to explain some of the problems with the current state of health insurance in the United States:

Insurance is supposed to provide us security and access to appropriate and necessary care when needed. Too often, stingy or poorly planned health insurance policies stand in the way of people getting the help they need for pain. Arguably, the financial cost to society through such consequences as loss of work time, reliance on emergency medical services, and treatment of substance abuse outweighs whatever savings the insurance companies realize through limiting payments for alternative pain therapies. Worse, the cost in human suffering is incalculable.[34]

Financial Problems

The combination of high medical bills and job loss or reduction can take a toll on a person's finances. Some people with chronic pain may find themselves facing bankruptcy—when they have to give up their possessions or a large part of their paycheck to settle their debts—or having to depend on public assistance such as food stamps and Medicaid to meet their most basic needs. Others are forced to drastically change their lifestyles in order to cut their expenses or increase their income, such as moving to a smaller home or having the healthier spouse take on a second job. These changes can lead to further stress and emotional issues.

Applying for Social Security Disability Insurance (SSDI) is an option for those who know they will never be able to work again. SSDI is a public assistance program that is paid for by taxes; a small portion of money is taken out of everyone's paycheck, and when someone needs that money, they are able to access it by applying and being approved for the program. However, it is often a long and frustrating process that involves proving they are truly disabled and therefore really need the money. It is not supposed to be used by people who are able to support themselves with a job.

Gurnett has been fighting for disability benefits for more than four years and believes the main problem is that his condition is invisible and he does not always look sick. He also feels judged for the limited hobbies he pursues to fill his time and keep his spirits up. Because he is able to push himself to do these

Chronic pain can cause a number of financial problems.

things sometimes, judges have argued, he should be able to push himself to hold down a job. "It's hard explaining to a judge that when I'm doing things that involve me getting out of my house … I'm not pretending that I'm sick; I'm pretending that I'm well," he said. "The courts appeared to want to punish me for being able to hold onto the last few things that I use to identify myself with."[35]

Some people are too embarrassed to ask for public assistance, as there is a stigma, or negative view, surrounding it. In many societies, people feel a person's worth is defined by whether they can take care of themselves and what kind of job they have. Many people believe those who receive public assistance are lazy and would prefer not to work, when in reality, many of them wish they could have a full-time job. This stigma is so strong that some people think it is acceptable to be rude to people who receive public assistance. This can cause negative emotional and psychological consequences for the person who is being targeted. Brandt explained,

> There's a … sense of shame for me (and for many others, I think) about admitting a disability. I just applied for SSDI, and it was depressing and a little embarrassing to do so. I'm depressed about it because I prefer to live in denial that this is going to be a long-lasting or permanent condition. And I'm embarrassed because even though rationally I know SSDI is an insurance policy that I paid into since I got my first job at age fourteen, it feels like asking for a handout.[36]

Impact on Society

Patients and their loved ones are not the only ones affected by chronic pain. Society as a whole is affected in many ways. As Webster wrote, "We truly have

The Funding Problem

Chronic pain conditions receive less money than more "popular" conditions when it comes to research into what causes them and how they might be treated. In 2013, the National Institutes of Health (NIH) spent approximately $475 million on pain treatment research, which makes up less than 1 percent of their total research spending that year.

Comparison of NIH Research Spending by Prevalence of Major Diseases

NIH FY2014 Research Spending (in Millions)

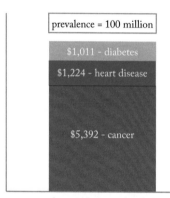

prevalence = 100 million

$1,011 - diabetes

$1,224 - heart disease

$5,392 - cancer

prevalence = 100 million

$402

cancer, heart disease, and diabetes   chronic pain

This information from the Chronic Pain Research Alliance shows the difference in spending on research for certain medical conditions in the 2014 fiscal year (FY2014). On these graphs, prevalence means the number of people with the conditions.

Because chronic pain is often misunderstood, it is easier for better-known conditions such as breast cancer to get federal funding, even though chronic pain affects a similar, if not larger, percentage of people. As Morris wrote, chronic pain "does not inspire telethons and rock concerts. There is simply nothing photogenic about an aching back that will not let you sleep, sit, travel ... and never stops hurting."[1] Supporters hope raising awareness of these conditions will also help raise funding.

1. David B. Morris, *The Culture of Pain*. Berkeley, CA: University of California Press, 1991, p. 66.

a problem with pain in our nation. *Crisis* is not too strong a word to put on it."[37] In terms of dollars, the IOM reported that "the annual national economic cost associated with chronic pain is estimated to be $560-635 billion."[38] This includes health care costs and productivity lost from people not being able to complete their work.

Chronic pain sufferers who are unable to work also lose tax dollars for their employers. The IOM reported that

> *people with severe pain missed an average of 5.0–5.9 more days of work per year than people with no pain … The cost of lost productivity included days of work missed ($11.6–12.7 billion), hours of work lost ($95.2–96.5 billion), and lost wages of ($190.6–226.3 billion).*[39]

Their family members can also lose productivity when they have to take time off to care for them.

Chronic pain sufferers need more health care than the average person, which results in higher costs for health care providers and insurance companies. According to the IOM, "on average, a person with moderate pain generates health care expenditures $4,516 higher than those for a person without pain. A person with severe pain generates health expenditures $3,210 higher than those for a person with moderate pain."[40] When things get really tough, people with chronic pain may need to rely on government programs. "The cost of pain to the federal government is immense,"[41] the IOM reported.

CHAPTER FOUR

TREATING CHRONIC PAIN

When it comes to treatment options, "chronic pain has no solution, just a collection of imperfect options."[42] Treatment is aimed at palliative care, which means finding ways to reduce and manage pain, rather than attempting to cure pain, which is currently not possible for most chronic pain conditions.

Medications

Scientific advances have led to a number of medication options for those seeking to treat different forms of chronic pain.

- *Basic pain relievers:* The most common form of pain relievers is analgesics, which affect the way pain messages are processed. These include over-the-counter nonsteroidal anti-inflammatory drugs (NSAIDs) such as aspirin, Ibuprofen, and Aleve. As the name suggests, NSAIDs relieve inflammation, which makes them good for treating arthritis,

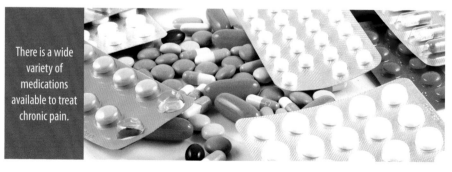

There is a wide variety of medications available to treat chronic pain.

back pain, and other sprains and cramps. NSAIDs are generally safe and are not addictive, but using them for long periods of time can cause digestive issues. They are best for mild to moderate pain; for moderate to severe pain, they may not be strong enough.

Other NSAIDs known as COX-2 inhibitors are believed to cause fewer digestive side effects, but their long-term side effects are not yet known and may cause increased risk for cardiovascular problems. As a result, they are best for patients who are already experiencing digestive issues and wish to avoid more. COX-2 inhibitors include prescription drugs such as Celebrex and Vioxx. Acetaminophen—most commonly known as Tylenol—is another over-the-counter medication useful for mild to moderate pain. It is generally safe, although long-term use could lead to liver damage. Patients on acetaminophen or NSAIDs for a long period of time should be monitored by their doctors for side effects.

Tramadol is a prescription pain medication that affects the way pain messages are processed. It also keeps brain hormones that decrease pain available to the brain for longer than normal. It is largely used for acute pain, but some chronic pain patients have found relief from it. As a result, it is worth mentioning as another tool in the pain relief toolkit. Immediate side effects can include drowsiness, dizziness, nausea, headache, and constipation. Long-term side effects may include tolerance, where a person needs a higher dose to achieve the same result, and physical dependence, where a person can become physically sick if they stop taking the drug. These can lead to addiction over a long enough time. Additionally, it may cause difficulty thinking and performing complex tasks, such as driving. For these reasons, many doctors prescribe Tramadol for short-term use only.

- *Antidepressants:* While they were created to treat depression and anxiety, antidepressants such as Elavil, Prozac, and Cymbalta can also affect the way pain messages are processed by the brain. They work best for pain caused by damaged nerves, fibromyalgia, and spinal cord injuries. Side effects can include drowsiness, weight gain, and dry mouth.

- *Anti-seizure medications:* In addition to preventing and controlling seizures, anti-seizure medications such as Gabapentin and Lamictal have also been shown to help reduce or stop the pain signals sent out by damaged nerves. Side effects can include drowsiness, dizziness, and nausea. In some patients, liver, heart, and blood disorders have occurred.

- *Stronger pain relievers:* When the above options are not strong enough, chronic pain sufferers may need to turn to stronger medications known as narcotics or opioids. Well-known opioids include hydrocodone, morphine, and oxycodone. Many of these are combined with other, weaker painkillers; for example, Lortab is a combination of hydrocodone and acetaminophen. Immediate side effects can include drowsiness, nausea, and constipation. However, by far the most concerning side effect for many doctors and patients is the risk of addiction.

According to the National Institute on Drug Abuse (NIDA), the United States is currently facing an opioid addiction epidemic. While in the past opioids were not believed to be addictive, that has been proven false. Research conducted between 2013 and 2016 found that between 21 and 29 percent of people who take opioids for chronic pain misuse them, and between 8 and 12 percent become addicted. To address this issue, doctors are starting to prescribe opioids less often, but this can harm people with chronic pain who cannot find relief with weaker painkillers. Medical experts are currently doing research into the problem to try to come up with a solution that minimizes the risk of addiction while still providing help to those who need it. As the IOM stated, "The majority of people with pain use their prescription drugs properly, are not a source of misuse, and should not be stigmatized or denied access because of the misdeeds or carelessness of others."[43]

It is important to note that while a chronic pain sufferer may become dependent on opioids, there is a difference between dependence and addiction. Dependence means the body becomes used to a drug and will feel symptoms of withdrawal if the person suddenly stops using it. However, the same could be said for diabetics who use insulin; just because the body relies on a drug to control symptoms, that does not mean the patient is addicted. Addiction occurs when a person feels driven to use opioids not for pain, but to achieve a high or for emotional comfort. People with an addiction generally experience an inability to stop using a drug even when it negatively affects their work or social life.

- *Injections:* Injecting medication directly into a pain site can also reduce pain. Steroids, anesthesia, and Botox are the most common substances injected for pain relief. In treatments called nerve blocks, anesthesia is injected directly into nerve fibers to stop pain signals from reaching the brain. With any injection, pain relief only lasts for a short period of time, at which point another injection is needed.

Celebrities and Chronic Pain

The fact that some wealthy celebrities suffer from chronic pain shows how difficult it is to treat. Many of them are able to afford the most cutting-edge treatments, yet they still experience pain. For example, Jillian Michaels has a line of fitness DVDs and helped people get healthy on *The Biggest Loser*. However, she suffers from endometriosis and polycystic ovary syndrome (PCOS)—a diagnosis she "kept ... to herself for years, worried that it would damage her 'beacon of health' reputation."[1]

More recently, Lady Gaga has opened up about her fibromyalgia, bringing attention to the issue of chronic pain. Her 2017 documentary, *Gaga: Five Foot Two*, aired on Netflix and detailed how her pain affects her professional and private life. Many people applauded Gaga for being willing to open up about her struggle in order to create awareness of chronic pain.

1. Bari Nan Cohen, "7 Celebrities Who Manage Life with Chronic Pain," *Prevention*, November 16, 2011. www.prevention.com/health/health-concerns/7-celebrities-who-manage-life-with-chronic-pain.

Non-Medication Treatments

For patients who do not want to take medication or who need something in addition to medication, there are other treatments that can help relieve or manage pain:

- *Topicals:* Topicals are pain medications that are applied to the skin. They include creams and gels such as capsaicin—the ingredient that makes chili peppers spicy—and methyl products such as Bengay and Icy Hot. Topicals are often used to relieve inflammation, muscle aches, and nerve pain. They work quickly to relieve mild pain but need to be reapplied frequently and are not effective for stronger, long-term pain.

- *Physical therapy:* Physical therapy is a treatment program that uses different techniques to reduce pain, build strength and endurance, and increase a patient's range of motion, or ability to move and function physically. While the goal is to "restore the body to its pre-pain condition," it can also be used to "rejuvenate [the] body so that it's less liable to hurt."[44] Even when physical therapy cannot "fix" a patient, it can still help relieve pain, increase their confidence, and prevent flare-ups, which are times when symptoms get significantly worse.

Physical therapy can help chronic pain patients move more easily.

- *Heat and cold therapy:* Applying heat or cold is something patients can do themselves, and it is safe and inexpensive compared to other treatment options. Cold treatments such as ice packs are useful for inflammation, mild joint pain, and headaches. Cold works by reducing blood flow to the pain site, creating a distracting pain signal, which causes pain signals to move to the brain at a slower speed. Heat treatments such as heating pads and hot baths are useful for stronger aches and pains in muscles and joints. Heat works to relieve pain by increasing blood flow and sending more nutrients to the pain site as well as improving flexibility. Patients can also find relief by alternating heat and cold.

- *TENS:* Transcutaneous electrical nerve stimulation (TENS) has been effective in relieving chronic pain in some patients, especially when used together with other treatments. TENS units work by placing small electrodes—electricity-conducting patches—on the skin near the pain site that send electrical impulses into the nerve pathway. Doctors are not certain how this relieves pain, although they have several theories: It may create "stop pain" signals, create a distraction from pain signals, cause muscles to relax, trigger the release of endorphins, or be a combination of two or more of those. A TENS unit is generally prescribed by a doctor.

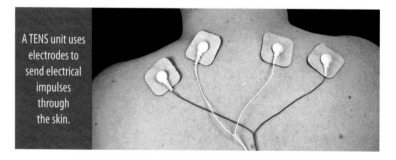

A TENS unit uses electrodes to send electrical impulses through the skin.

- *Surgery:* Surgery is rarely the best option for chronic pain sufferers. It is not effective for many forms of chronic pain, it can be risky, and it may cause brand-new pain issues. In many cases, it is only worth considering when all else has failed.

Complementary and Alternative Medicine

Treatments and therapies that are not practiced by traditional doctors are known as complementary and alternative medicine (CAM). These therapies can be used as an alternative to traditional medicine or in addition to it. Many have been used for thousands of years, but they have become increasingly popular in recent decades as people take their health care into their own hands and search for new ways to manage their pain. According to Laurie Edwards,

> *[Often,] the decision to try out CAM techniques comes after a long, frustrating trial-and-error existence within the confines of conventional medicine. When nothing else has worked, there is much less to risk losing, especially when relief is nowhere to be found. That is why CAM is so appealing to the millions of people living with constant pain and ongoing symptoms.*[45]

Some CAM treatments are more effective than others. Many that seem promising have simply not been studied enough to be proven effective, although there are plenty of firsthand reports from those who practice these techniques stating they have seen positive changes from them. While "[d]octors who recommend [CAM] don't contend [argue] that every form of complementary medicine is legitimate ... they do suggest that some CAM approaches to pain relief may be worth exploring."[46] Popular CAM approaches include:

- Chiropractors who stretch or adjust joints in order to relieve pain and encourage healing. Some studies have shown chiropractic treatment to be effective for lower back pain. While its usefulness is still up for debate, it is "perhaps the most commonly used alternative therapy in the United States,"[47] although it is difficult to say this with complete certainty, as exact numbers are unavailable.

- Massage is an ancient practice in which a massage therapist applies pressure to different parts of the body in order to move the patient's muscles and soft tissues. Massage has been found to have a number of positive effects, including lower blood pressure, increased range of motion, and stress relief. Massage is fairly safe, although patients with inflammation or circulation problems may want to check with their doctors first.

- Yoga is another ancient practice that dates back 5,000 years. Students follow yoga teachers (or instructional videos) to do a series of postures while carefully breathing in and out. These postures stretch the body, strengthen muscles, and are believed to help improve phsyical, mental, and emotional health. Many studies support yoga's ability to help people control their pain and decrease their stress when practiced regularly. A good yoga teacher can help students with chronic pain conditions adjust their poses as needed to avoid injury.

Yoga can improve flexibility, strengthen muscles, and make people feel calmer.

- Tai chi is a series of slow, graceful movements designed to increase flexibility, balance, coordination, and muscle strength. Because it is slow and low-impact, it is easier for chronic pain sufferers than other forms of exercise. It has been shown to help with conditions such as arthritis, fibromyalgia, and some headaches. It can also decrease stress, ease depression, and help with sleep.

- Acupuncture involves the insertion of 1 to 10 extremely thin needles into specific areas in a patient's skin. These needles are kept in place for anywhere from 15 to 40 minutes and are not supposed to hurt. While not many studies have been done on acupuncture's effectiveness, the NIH has said it can help relieve nausea, back pain, osteoarthritis, fibromyalgia, and migraines. Acupuncture is relatively safe, although patients should make sure their acupuncturist is following safety procedures such as using clean needles for each patient.

- Meditation is something people can learn from a teacher, mental health care provider, book, podcast, or other instructional material. There are many different forms of meditation, but at its simplest it means finding a quiet spot where one can sit for a period of time and clear the mind of thoughts. This is done by focusing on one's breathing and doing a simple task that helps to focus the mind, such as repeating a saying over and over or imagining a scene such as a relaxing beach. At first, meditation may feel incredibly difficult as the mind likes to wander, but with practice, it gets easier. Meditation has been found to relieve stress, anxiety, and pain. Mindfulness is a type of meditative practice

Meditation can be done anywhere that is quiet and free of interruptions.

that involves clearing the mind and focusing on the senses by making basic observations about the present moment without judging anything. "I focus on all the little things around me," Fudalik said, "the sight, smell, feel, sound, taste of things (although I make sure to only focus on external feelings since my body hurts). When I go into sensory overload, which happens easily, I make sure I have areas of the house I can escape to that are quiet with little light and as comfortable a chair or bed as I can get."[48]

- Progressive muscle relaxation involves focusing on tensing up different parts of the body, holding that tension for a count of several seconds, and then releasing it, all while carefully breathing in and out. This is repeated for every area of the body from the top of the head down to the soles of the feet.

- Hypnosis may sound like a magic trick, but it is actually an ancient practice used by professionals—from mental health providers to dentists whose patients cannot tolerate traditional painkillers. Hypnosis puts the patient's mind in a relaxed state so they are open to suggestion—specifically, suggestions that give them the power to decrease their pain and increase their ability to manage pain. While the patient must be willing to undergo hypnosis in order for it to work, the Mayo Clinic reported in 1999 that "about 80 percent of adults can be hypnotized by a trained professional."[49] Hypnosis has been proven relatively effective; one study found it helped reduce 75 percent of patients' pain.

There are many other CAM practices that have less evidence to back them up. While those who follow these practices may report positive effects, there is little to no scientific evidence to prove them, and some can actually be harmful. These include:

- *Aromatherapy:* Using essential oils from plants has been reported to promote positive feelings and relieve pain. While this may be relaxing, there are no proven scientific benefits. However, unless someone is allergic to a particular scent, it is not harmful either, and reducing stress can help reduce pain.

- *Supplements:* Supplements are pills, capsules, and tablets made from herbs and minerals aimed at relieving specific symptoms and conditions. Unlike traditional drugs, supplements are not inspected by the government to make sure they are safe and effective. Some patients may find them useless; others may actually experience negative side effects or interactions with other medication they are taking. It is always best to check with a doctor before taking any supplements.

- *Magnet therapy:* Some people believe the magnetic fields present in everything have an effect on human bodies. They recommend wearing magnets or putting magnets in things such as pillows or car seat covers to increase healing and decrease pain. Studies on magnet therapy have had mixed results. In some cases, they may actually have negative side effects—for instance, if the person is pregnant or has a medical implant such as a pacemaker. People who experience chronic pain should not try any treatment they have not first discussed with their doctor.

Medical Marijuana

While medical marijuana is not legal nationally, it is currently legal in 29 U.S. states and Washington, D.C. Marijuana comes from the cannabis plant and has been used for more than 12,000 years. It has been proven useful for pain conditions such as fibromyalgia, headaches, arthritis, and CFS. Pain relief is actually the most common reason patients use medical marijuana, according to a survey by the International Association for Cannabinoid Medicines (IACM).

Gurnett found that medical marijuana is the only thing that helps him with some of his symptoms:

I have had chronic nausea for 20 years. I have tried every possible medication to fix this problem. I've been to a gastroenterologist [doctor who specializes in the digestive system] who literally told me that there was nothing wrong and a neurologist [doctor who specializes in the nerves and brain] who just sent me to a pain management specialist. Before medical marijuana, I could go days without eating and I woke up every morning with a pain that is best described as shattered glass in my stomach. With medical marijuana, I wake up every day without that pain. I don't have to worry about [whether] I will be able to eat, or when.[50]

Medical marijuana products can be smoked, taken in foods, dissolved as a liquid placed under the tongue, inhaled as vapor, or applied directly to the skin. Side effects are mild when used moderately, but higher doses may result in feelings of anxiety, confusion, and panic. With 27 varieties of cannabis that can be used medically, different strains of marijuana can be used to help with different symptoms. However, marijuana should never be used in places where it is illegal, and it should generally be avoided by people under the age of 18, as it can have harmful effects on developing brains.

Trial and Error: Finding What Works

Different people react to medication differently. Everything from how the body absorbs medication to what side effects it causes depends on each person's unique chemical makeup. As a result, "There's no good way to predict how you'll respond to a certain medication … other than to give it a try,"[51] according to Dr. Perry Fine, former associate medical director of the University of Idaho Pain Management Center.

In addition, people with the same condition may experience different symptoms. Some migraine patients see an aura—strange visual effects—before they get a migraine, for instance, while others do not. Some migraine patients discover that caffeine triggers their migraine attacks, while for others, caffeine prevents their attacks. As a result, each patient's treatment plan must be created with their specific needs in mind. Even when a patient has a diagnosis, finding effective treatment is often a matter of trial and error, which can become frustrating and discouraging. As the IOM reported, "Many patients are not told, or do not readily comprehend, that the road to finding the right combination of treatments for them may be a long one with many different approaches to treatment until the right match is found."[52]

Counseling and Mind-Body Therapies

Since emotions and thoughts play a large role in how pain is experienced, some patients "can use the inner power of [their] mind to control—or at least change—the intensity or quality of pain, even if the pain doesn't entirely go away."[53] Counseling and mind-body therapies aim to help people do this. They have been shown to reduce pain, lower stress, relieve depression, and boost confidence. Popular mind-body therapies include the following:

- Cognitive-behavioral therapy (CBT) teaches people to cope with negative emotions in healthy ways. They learn to identify their harmful thoughts and emotions and reframe them with more positive thoughts. For instance, instead of thinking, "I feel terrible today," a patient may remind themselves, "Tomorrow is another day, and it's okay if I need to rest today. Focusing on how bad I feel won't make things better." They also learn skills such as how to relax and how to set more realistic goals. Having a therapist can also give a chronic pain patient someone to talk to besides their friends and family. While a strong network of loved ones is important and friends and family should be willing to listen, hearing about nothing but the person's pain for a long time can frustrate loved ones. Speaking to a therapist prevents a

Talking with a counselor or therapist can help chronic pain patients learn to deal with their symptoms.

chronic pain patient from making their loved ones their only source of support.

- Biofeedback uses sensors placed on a patient to provide feedback on physical activity such as heart rate, breathing rate, blood pressure, and how tense their muscles are. The therapist leads the patient through relaxation techniques. By watching the way these techniques affects their body, the patient learns how to put themselves in a calm state that helps them deal with—and maybe even reduce—their pain.

- Distraction, or finding something else to focus on, does more than just take a person's mind off their pain; it can actually "run interference on pain and make the gate swing further closed."[54] Because the nervous system can only handle a certain amount of signals at once, a person's thoughts and physical experiences can compete with pain signals and trick the brain into ignoring these signals. Listening to music has been shown to reduce stress, relieve pain, and improve a person's mood. Art can also provide healing, as well as a sense of productivity and satisfaction. "I used to be heavily into art," Fudalik said. "Since my hands are too shaky now, and sitting for long periods is hard, I now engage in a variety of crafts. I find the activity itself relaxing, a distraction from pain, and I feel I'm accomplishing something since there's a tangible end product, even if I can only work on a project for five minutes in a week."[55]

- Laughter or humor therapy distracts people from their pain and has been shown to have positive effects on the body. One study performed in the early 2000s found that people who watched a comedian perform "showed significant improvement in immune system functions."[56] In another, "just anticipating a humorous video boosted subjects' moods and made them less tense."[57] There are even clubs such as the World Laughter Tour, in which participants perform various stretching movements while clapping their hands and saying, "Ho-ho, ha-ha-ha."

- Emotional support animals such as dogs and cats can also help chronic pain sufferers deal with their emotions. Research has shown that interacting with an animal can reduce stress and lower blood pressure. "One study found that elderly people with pets visit the doctor less than petless peers. Another found that people released from coronary treatment at a hospital survived longer on average if they had pets."[58] Kassler gets comfort from her family's dog and a cat she obtained as emotional support animals: "My golden retriever knows when I'm upset and does her best to comfort me by lying next to me. My cat follows me everywhere and loves to cuddle. These instances of care calm me down and help me to focus on their support rather than the pain."[59]

Animals such as dogs and cats can provide chronic pain sufferers with comfort and companionship.

Lifestyle Changes

Changing certain daily habits can also help chronic pain sufferers. As the Mayo Clinic advised, "Managing chronic pain isn't about making your pain disappear. It's about learning how to keep your pain at a tolerable level. It's about enjoying life again, despite your pain."[60] The main types of lifestyle changes that can help with chronic pain are diet and exercise.

Some people with chronic pain benefit from a change in diet. IBS patients, for instance, should avoid fatty foods and eat a lot of small meals throughout the day rather than three big ones. Mitochondrial myopathy symptoms may be eased by eating complex carbohydrates and high-protein meals, which are digested more slowly and give the body energy longer. It is always best to check with a doctor before starting a new diet; there are many "miracle diets" advertised that have no scientific proof of helping with chronic pain.

While exercise can be challenging for people who suffer from chronic pain, getting some form of physical activity each day is recommended to keep the body healthy and make pain easier to manage. Physical activity has a number of benefits, including reducing stress, releasing endorphins, strengthening muscles, increasing heart and lung strength, and controlling weight. It can also relieve stress and help people sleep better. In contrast, inactivity can lead to conditions such as heart disease, diabetes, high cholesterol, and added stress on the body, which can make pain harder to manage. Studies have shown even healthy people's bodies begin to decline after a few weeks of inactivity. To get as many health benefits as possible, it is best to include a variety of different exercises every day: stretching, range-of-motion exercises that help with flexibility; strength-building exercises such as lifting light weights; aerobic activity, or things that increase the heart rate and breathing; and practicing good posture.

Exercising with Chronic Pain

"Bed rest is seldom recommended anymore, even for people experiencing pain,"[1] advised the late Dr. Richard Materson of the University of Texas Medical School at Houston and Baylor College of Medicine. Exercise is important to keep the body in good working order and prevent pain from getting worse. However, chronic pain sufferers can find it hard to exercise. They tire easily and worry about hurting themselves more. They must learn how to get exercise in small, easy doses by:

- *keeping it moderate*: Exercise has benefits even it is something easy on the body, such as walking around the block. Just half an hour of moderate physical activity several times a week can make a positive difference.

- *setting smaller goals*: If half an hour is too much, exercise can be broken into smaller time blocks such as 10 or 15 minutes repeated throughout the day.

- *getting a doctor's approval*: Some physical activity may be better for a chronic pain sufferer than others, depending on their personal history and health issues. It is always best to check with a doctor first before trying anything new.

- *starting small*: Start off doing only a small amount of exercise at first, and only increase when the body shows it can tolerate it. Pacing and not overdoing it are key.

1. Quoted in Richard Laliberte, *Doctors' Guide to Chronic Pain: The Newest, Quickest, and Most Effective Ways to Find Relief.* Pleasantville, NY: The Reader's Digest Association, Inc., 2003, p. 103.

Other important lifestyle changes that can help with chronic pain include:

- *Stress management:* Stress can make existing physical and emotional conditions worse, so finding ways to relax is important for managing pain. Activities such as yoga, meditation, doing hobbies, or hanging out with friends are some of the many ways to unwind and manage stress.

- *Energy management:* Because people with chronic pain often have a smaller energy supply than most, it is important for them to learn how to use their energy in the smartest way possible. Keeping a journal can be useful to record things such as daily pain levels, activities, mood, and

Planning out each day's activities can help pain sufferers use their limited energy smartly.

sleep. This can help them identify patterns and things that trigger a flare-up of symptoms. "I try to keep my body within its limits but not get too lazy since that causes pain as well," Fudalik said. "I also plan out my many hobbies and household chores; everything is listed out. I consider what my body is capable of on the best and worst days ... A day where I am seeing a friend or going to the grocery store will be the only thing on my list since either of those activities takes the rest of the day, sometimes the day after and day after that, to recover from."[61]

- *Adjusting expectation:* Living with chronic pain means learning to let go of unrealistic expectations and to accept and work within the body's limits. People must let go of trying to "do it all" or be perfect and instead "[b]ecome a perfectionist at adjusting [their] goals."[62]

- *Creating structure:* Chronic pain (and, for some, the lack of a regular job) can make the hours and days blur together. Making sure each day has a mix of activities in it can help create a sense of purpose and meaning. This includes things such as rest, work—a job, chores, etc.— exercise, play, and time with friends and family.

CHAPTER FIVE

THE TROUBLE WITH "INVISIBLE ILLNESSES"

Chronic pain sufferers face a unique challenge because their conditions are mostly "invisible illnesses." Unlike a broken leg or the measles, pain is not something other people can see unless a person behaves in a way that clearly shows they are in pain—moaning, crying, etc. To make things more confusing, many chronic pain sufferers are very good at hiding their pain for a number of reasons, such as not wanting to worry people or to seem like they are complaining. Fudalik explained,

> *Because I put all my energy into the times I'm with family and friends and pull out my best acting skills to seem normal, only those closest to me really see how I am every day. Those of us with chronic illnesses are constantly trying our best to seem healthy in public, even if it means coming home and knowing you'll have days of utter pain, fatigue, mental functioning problems, and a multitude of other symptoms flaring up.*[63]

Susan Wendell, who has ME/CFS, wrote about how people have trouble remembering a person with an invisible illness is disabled: "To be recognized as disabled, we have to remind people frequently of our needs and limitations. That in itself can be a source of alienation from other people ... because it requires repeatedly calling attention to our impairments."[64] As a result, friends and loved ones often have no idea how serious a chronic pain sufferer's condition really is. This can lead to a number of problems.

"But You Don't Look Sick!"

One of the most frustrating things for a chronic pain sufferer to hear is, "But you don't look sick!" While the person who says this may be trying to offer a compliment or express their surprise, it often makes the chronic pain sufferer feel as though the person is downplaying how serious their pain really is. Telaak explained,

> I hear "you don't look sick" more often than I can count, and that one in particular makes me want to crawl out of my skin when I am feeling my worst. I think it's hard for people to empathize when they haven't been through this type of pain before ... I look very healthy; someone from the outside looking at me could never guess everything my body has been through thanks to my illnesses, and unless I'm in a bathing suit you wouldn't see the mess of scars on my abdomen.[65]

Because chronic pain sufferers often try to hide how much pain they are in, they can also feel dismissed by people when they do reveal how they are feeling. When someone with CFS describes how exhausted they are, for instance, a friend who does not understand the condition might wave off their feelings by saying, "Oh, we're all tired!" However, a normal person's feeling of tiredness and a CFS patient's exhaustion are two very different things. This is another reason people with chronic pain tend to keep their feelings to themselves.

Telaak said that people who think they have experienced similar pain or that she is exaggerating her pain add to the emotional distress caused by her physical symptoms:

> I think people who see my pain as normal menstrual pain or think I'm weak because I can't handle normal pain are the hardest to process. It's incredibly upsetting because I have a condition that has been confirmed through surgery. I also have a surprisingly

Chronic pain sufferers often keep their feelings from their friends and family because they do not want to face negative reactions.

high pain tolerance, so the fact that it can double me over and make me sick to my stomach is not normal. I understand women have menstrual pain, but I don't think most of them are up at 2:00 in the morning throwing up because their pain is so intense.[66]

For Sean Bishop, who suffers from fibromyalgia, the hardest thing is when those closest to him see him in pain every day but still do not believe him:

I have spent the last 18 years of my life trying to convince my parents that I'm sicker than they think I am. They either don't ask how I'm feeling, or when they do, they downplay how sick I'm telling them I am. I've had them come to doctor's visits with me, I've given them books on my illness ... While I think they're trying to understand, they still have an uncanny knack for finding the smallest, most insulting thing that they can say to me, and I don't even think they realize they're doing it half the time. Sometimes I wonder if it's all because they're in denial that I'm sick, and that makes them feel better.[67]

While some people have trouble understanding how sick a chronic pain sufferer really is, others have trouble seeing a chronic pain patient as anything other than a chronic pain patient. It can be just as frustrating for someone with chronic pain to be left out of plans, underestimated, or treated as fragile because they are sick. Telaak described the way she wished to be treated:

The Spoon Theory

The Spoon Theory was created by Christine Miserandino, who suffers from lupus, an autoimmune disease (a disease that causes the body to attack itself). She runs the website But You Don't Look Sick. One day, while eating at a diner with a friend, Miserandino gave her friend 12 spoons to represent how much energy she had available within a day. As her friend described each activity she would do in a normal day—showering, getting dressed, cooking meals—Miserandino took away a spoon for each one.

Her friend quickly realized that, with only so many spoons to use each day, she'd have to decide which activities were the most important and let everything else go. She could try to do more by "borrowing" spoons from the next day, but that would mean she'd have fewer spoons the following day, and the day after that would be even harder. The only real way to get spoons back is to rest and recharge.

The Spoon Theory has become popular with many chronic illness communities, as it can be hard for people with chronic pain to get loved ones to understand why they often need to rest and cannot do as many things as they would like to. Some members call themselves "Spoonies," and there is a growing amount of Spoonie merchandise, including shirts and coffee mugs, for sale online.

I wish there was more human kindness around chronic pain. Instead of judging situations they don't understand, I wish more people would assume innocence and try to think what it would be like to have an illness rather than write someone off because of it. I also wish more people knew how capable we are. Just because we battle this pain and are sometimes limited by it doesn't mean we aren't valuable.[68]

Bad or Unwanted Advice

People with chronic pain can be frustrated when they receive advice from friends and loved ones, even if that advice is well meant. Since most people are only familiar with acute pain, which can be fixed by doing the right things, their advice to chronic pain sufferers may not be useful. It can also come across as insulting; it implies that the chronic pain sufferer is not doing enough or trying hard enough to make themselves better. One thing that especially upsets Fudalik is "people who can't believe I'm not better yet. Many people don't understand that there's no miracle cure (despite all the articles they find on the internet)."[69]

McLaughlin voiced the same frustration:

> *The fact that you're just not going to get better seems unbelievable to most people ... It's easier for them to believe that there is something you can control ... There must be something you can do that you aren't doing! Eating raw foods, forcing yourself to exercise, thinking your way out of it, trying the latest drugs that promise a cure in their commercial: something should work, and if you're not better, then you're not working hard enough. It's frustrating, it's everywhere (even, sometimes, in my own mind), and it's just wrong. It's just wrong: I can't think or eat or exercise my way out of these illnesses, no matter how hard I try.*[70]

It can also be hard for chronic pain sufferers to tell whether the advice they find through their own research is good or bad. Treatments that may work for one person may not work for others, and other treatments, such as some CAM therapies, may not be proven to work at all. Discovering what works and what does not can take years and lead to frustration and loss of hope. "The consuming nature of severe pain leads people down many pathways in search of information, ideas, and of

Loved ones' advice, while well-meaning, may not always be helpful or accurate.

course relief of pain," the IOM wrote. "As a result, suffering individuals are likely to receive conflicting and outdated information and advice that are not applicable to their individual situation, and may also be exposed to myths about pain and its treatment."[71] Or, as the Mayo Clinic put it, "Anyone who has the necessary hardware and software can publish a Web page or offer medical advice. And the Internet has a way of making all health information appear equal."[72]

Judgment

A better understanding of what causes pain has helped erase some mistaken notions about pain, such as the idea that it is a punishment for being a bad person. However, chronic pain sufferers still face misunderstanding and judgment because their symptoms cannot be seen easily. Western society is one "that values youth, physical fitness, and overachievement,"[73] and when a person is not able to live up to those standards, people may look down on them. In addition, "Americans today probably belong to the first generation on earth that looks at a pain-free life as something like a constitutional right. Pain is [considered] a scandal ... We are not well equipped for what happens when our pills fail."[74] As a result, it can be hard for people to understand why someone is not getting better—which can lead to the mistaken belief that they are not doing everything they can. "If we could choose a different way, we would sign up in a heartbeat," Telaak said, "but our illness is not a choice, and thus we shouldn't be judged for it."[75]

Chronic pain sufferers also face judgment from people who do not understand why they act sick when they look fine on the outside. Fudalik explained,

> *When you use a cane, wheelchair, even a brace in public, people are much more helpful and understanding if you have trouble moving. When I go*

out without some physical sign of my illness, people get disgusted and angry when I move slowly, when I stumble and even fall in store aisles and parking lots. They get mad if I don't give up a seat for someone else, or when I need to just put my head down at a restaurant table because I'm overwhelmed by all the sensory input, fatigue, and pain.[76]

Kate Eastman, who suffers from ME/CFS, wrote on The Mighty,

I received a disability parking permit this week ... but I'm currently too scared to use it. Too scared to face the condemning looks as I step out of the car and walk without visible impairment into the shops. Too scared to hear the words, "But you are not disabled!" shouted across the parking lot.[77]

Since chronic pain symptoms vary from day to day, people may be confused about how sick a person really is. This leads to a no-win situation; if someone stays in to rest, they are labeled as lazy. If they push themselves to go out and do things, people assume they cannot really be that sick. Tressia Demaskie, who suffers from fibromyalgia and chronic back pain, wrote on The Mighty, "I'm just trying to 'live,' I'm not asking to be judged. Instead of judging me for enjoying a day of shopping, praise me for putting both feet on the floor each morning, a smile on my face and going when my body wanted to stay in bed."[78]

Problems with Doctors

While chronic pain sufferers might understand why friends and loved ones have trouble understanding their condition, many are surprised by how many medical professionals have trouble, too. Plenty of patients have had bad experiences with doctors who doubted their symptoms, thought they were exaggerating, or gave up on exploring new treatment options after too many attempts failed. "The bad experiences were crushing,"Telaak said. "I would go home and feel so defeated. It's one thing to have to deal with how chronic pain wreaks havoc on your life, but it's another thing to be in the eye of the storm and feel like you've been abandoned by modern medicine."[79] Lisa Prins, who suffers from renal tubular acidosis, among other conditions, wrote on The Mighty,

> *Patients are often presumed healthy until they "prove" otherwise. Because they are presumed healthy, they have to jump through hoops just to get a test done or get a referral to a specialist. It's a never-ending fight to be treated with dignity, caring and respect.*[80]

Doctors' inability to handle chronic pain properly can be traced back to the fact that it is "among the most difficult medical conditions to treat."[81] Since there is no official way to measure it and each person experiences pain differently, it can be hard to trust a patient's own description of their pain. It can also be frustrating to be faced with a patient whose symptoms are hard to pin down and who does not seem to be responding to treatment. Doctors such as primary care physicians may not have the training necessary to treat someone with chronic pain, yet *The Journal of the American Medical Association (JAMA)* reported that "[o]nly a quarter of people with moderate to severe chronic pain ever get a referral to a pain specialist."[82] One reason is that there are far more people in pain than there are specialists.

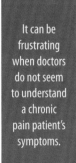

It can be frustrating when doctors do not seem to understand a chronic pain patient's symptoms.

As the IOM found at the time of its report, "There are more than 28,500 people with chronic pain for every specialist."[83]

If a patient is unhappy with a doctor's treatment and searches for another doctor—or if they visit a number of doctors hoping to find one they like—they may be labeled as difficult, causing future doctors to mistrust them or refuse to see them at all. "Patients on average have seen five or six doctors before they get to us," said pain specialist Dr. Vildan Mullin. "Some patients have seen as many as 15 different doctors."[84] Although the process is often stressful, finding a good doctor can be life-changing. Telaak explained her feelings of relief and gratitude the first time she met a doctor who took her seriously:

> *I cried … I was in his office for an hour talking, and … I knew he cared and was invested. This was over 12 years after I spoke with my first doctor about my pain. I think many of the doctors dismissed me because I was young or thought that I was exaggerating my pain. It was so vindicating to both have someone take me seriously, then to have my condition confirmed through the surgery.*[85]

Women and Pain

Women with chronic pain face an added layer of misunderstanding. Studies suggest "women tend to feel pain more intensely than men do."[86] Everything from hormones to height and weight differences may be behind this. Studies have also shown that medication can affect men and women differently, meaning a painkiller that helps a male patient may not work for a female patient. Part of the issue is the way society views gender roles, or the ways men and women are expected to behave. Men are expected to be strong at all times, which may lead some of them to keep quiet about their pain or describe it as being better than it is. In contrast, women are "allowed" to be more vocal about their pain, which means they are more likely to seek treatment and take pain medication.

The "Smiley Face" Pain Scale

Chronic pain cannot be measured, but some medical providers try by asking patients to describe their pain on a scale of 0 (no pain at all) to 10 (worst pain imaginable). However, this scale can be frustrating for chronic pain sufferers. Each person experiences pain differently, and chronic pain patients experience it on a different level than average patients. For example, what an average person might rate as a 6, a chronic pain patient might rate as a 3 because their version of a 6 is much more intense. This means a chronic pain patient might unintentionally be undervaluing their own pain, making a doctor think it is not as bad as it really is.

Because of the difficulties involved with this type of pain scale, many people prefer the comparative pain scale. Instead of simple descriptive phrases such as "unbearable" or "distressing" or trying to match a patient's facial expression to a simply drawn face, this type of scale goes into detail about what the pain feels like. For example, number 3 on this scale describes "tolerable" pain as "Very noticeable pain, like an accidental cut, blow to the nose causing a bloody nose, or doctor giving you an injection. The pain is not so strong that you cannot get used to it."[1] In contrast, number 6, or "intense" pain, is described as "Strong, deep, piercing pain [like a] bad headache, several bee stings, or a bad back pain. So strong it seems to partially dominate your senses, causing you to think somewhat unclearly."[2] This type of detail helps doctors more clearly understand how much pain their patient is in.

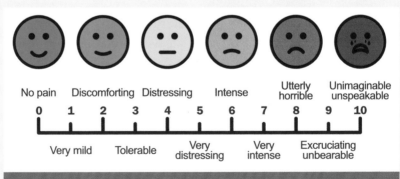

The 0 to 10 pain scale found in health care providers' offices can be hard to answer for patients with chronic pain.

1. Alice Rich, "0–10 Pain Scale," Lucile Packard Children's Hospital Heart Center/CVICU, last updated May 2014. www.gpscbc.ca/sites/default/files/uploads/Pain_082.0_Comparative_Pain_Scale_PR.pdf.

2. Rich, "0–10 Pain Scale."

Finding the Right Doctor

There is nothing wrong with trying multiple doctors to find the one who fits best. Finding the right doctor is key when it comes to patients finding the best treatments to manage their chronic pain. Signs a doctor is a bad fit include:

- They are not willing to listen.
- They doubt the patient's honesty.
- They shut down questions or disagreements.
- They are not willing to explain things.
- They seem cold, rude, or bored.
- They do not seem knowledgeable about the condition.
- They act like they know everything even when they are wrong.
- They rush through appointments.

However, society's expectations for women also make them less likely to be taken seriously when they talk about their pain. Historically, there is a "caricature of women as delicate, emotional, and prone to difficult-to-understand whims," said Dr. Sarah Whitman, a psychiatrist who specializes in working with people in pain. "So it's easier to just dismiss their pain complaint as 'it can't be that bad,' or, 'she's just overreacting.'"[87] Further, since men are often taught to "suck it up" and be strong, when a man complains of pain, "he's more likely to be taken seriously because doctors assume he'd only speak up if it was really bad."[88]

While women experience more pain than men, they often have trouble getting doctors to take their symptoms seriously.

Women and men also communicate differently, with men tending to describe things in analytic terms ("there's a stabbing feeling in my right arm"), while women tend to describe things in emotional terms ("I feel miserable"). Because of this, women are more likely to have their pain dismissed as an emotional problem rather than a physical problem. One survey found that women were 37 percent more likely to be prescribed anti-anxiety medication and 82 percent more likely to be prescribed an antidepressant for pain than men with the same diagnosis. This can be very frustrating and discouraging for female pain patients.

Although gender roles do play a part in the way men and women experience pain, there is more to it than that. Within the last few years, researchers have discovered that cells called glia, which are immune-like cells in the brain and spinal cord, play a role in the way women experience pain. Glia "are critical for the health and well-being of our brains and are known to contribute to several neurological diseases."[89] Although scientists have known for some time that they contribute to chronic pain, it is only recently that they have studied the way glia and biological sex are connected. They found that the pain women experience "is fundamentally different to male pain owing to the different reliance on glia. The result is that women's experience of pain is more severe than men's and the pain is harder to treat."[90] With this knowledge, researchers can try to develop drugs that target glia, potentially leading to more effective pain relief for women.

The Importance of Self-Advocacy

To get the best medical treatment possible, it is important for chronic pain sufferers to learn to practice self-advocacy, or "the ability ... to communicate, convey, negotiate, or assert his or her interests, desires, needs, and rights."[91] In other words, they must be willing to stand up for themselves and understand that they are ultimately responsible for their success when it comes to managing their pain.

Gurnett, who runs a support group for young adults with chronic pain, often sees this firsthand. He said,

> *In a time where people seem to be more and more critical of the services they receive—like going to a restaurant, for example—it seems that people are still hesitant to question their doctors' opinions or just to understand that they can switch doctors if they need to. For some, I think it's ... that they don't have the energy to challenge it anymore. Advocacy is the most important thing you can do for yourself as a patient because you need to understand that nobody cares about you more than you.*[92]

As Paula Nuschke Alford, who lives with several chronic pain conditions, put it, "You get to the point where you say, 'Hey, I've gotta help myself here. I've gotta become a fighter, and I have to really find strategies to take care of myself.'"[93]

Self-advocacy can be difficult at first because people are used to the idea that their doctor knows everything, and some doctors encourage this view by not admitting when they are wrong or unsure about something. Patients who practice self-advocacy learn everything they can about their conditions and which treatment options are available to them. They ask questions when visiting doctors and are not afraid to speak up when a doctor says or does something that does not seem right to them. They also resolve to make changes in their lives that will help them manage their pain and keep their spirits up. As a result, self-advocacy not only helps a patient get better treatment, it also boosts their confidence and helps them feel they are more in control of their condition.

The Role of Support Groups

Many people with chronic pain benefit from joining some type of support group. In a support group, they are able to meet with other chronic pain sufferers who understand what they are going through and can offer encouragement and useful advice to help each other cope. In a support group, members can be honest about their feelings and struggles without fear of judgment. They find a sense of belonging and hope by having the chance to get out of the house and connect with others who understand what it is like to live with chronic pain.

Gurnett created his own support group when he found that the support groups in his area did not meet his needs:

> *I experienced deep isolation after I got my diagnosis and I found it was really hard meeting other people with illnesses. I think that younger people go through some different issues than older people go through. There are a lot that are similar, but I feel it's much harder getting struck with an illness when you're in the prime of your life. Usually when I would go to support groups with older people in them, they were very depressing and I didn't think they were doing enough to try and uplift each other.*[94]

He started a combination support group and game night for young adults with invisible illnesses on the website Meetup, and 2 years later, it meets twice a month and includes about 85 members.

Those who do not have support groups in their area or cannot get out of the house to attend a local group can connect with other chronic pain sufferers online through social media, forums, and other resources. Brandt explained how important blogging has been to her since she started experiencing chronic pain:

> *It's a safe space for me to examine … my mystery illness … and talk about how it has affected me and*

*my family emotionally, without feeling like I'm put-
ting too big a burden on any one person by confiding
in them ... I hear from people who suffer similar
symptoms, or love someone who does, and they share
their diagnoses with me, the treatments that have
been helpful and those that weren't.*[95]

Having a strong support system of friends and family has been shown to help people cope better with
their pain, lower their stress, and prevent them from
developing depression. It also has physical benefits such
as boosting the immune system, lowering blood pressure and cholesterol, and helping people live longer.
However, even caring, helpful loved ones can have trouble relating to what a chronic pain sufferer lives with on
a daily basis. Support groups provide this understanding. Telaak explained,

*Finding forums online was a turning point for me.
For the first time, I felt the validation of knowing
what I was living with was absolutely not normal. Now that I have a group that I meet up with
in person, I feel even more supported. Words can't
describe how impactful it has been to have people
to be around who understand living with chronic
pain. I can let my guard completely down with my
fellow chronic pain sufferers.*[96]

Loved ones may also benefit from joining a support group. Because someone with chronic pain often
needs extra help and support, their caregivers—those
closest to them who help them most frequently—may

Support groups
provide chronic
pain sufferers with
understanding,
encouragement,
and a sense
of belonging.

sometimes experience stress or other negative emotions. Just because someone is relatively healthy does not mean they are unstoppable; they also sometimes get minor illnesses or experience frustration or depression. Additionally, someone with a mental illness such as anxiety or bipolar disorder may be a caretaker for someone with a physical illness. It is important for caregivers, no matter what their level of health is, not to ignore their own needs while caring for a loved one. In an article for the *Huffington Post*, Lee Woodruff, who cares for her husband who was injured in Iraq, explained the importance of self-care for caregivers:

> *I know all too well that being a family caregiver can be a demanding job. Some days, you may feel like you can do anything, and others, you may not be sure how you'll get through the day. To be an effective caregiver for someone else, you must first take care of yourself. Make sure to get enough rest, eat right, and exercise … It's also critical to allow others to provide a support system, and don't be afraid to ask for help.[97]*

When a caregiver sees the amount of pain their loved one is in on a regular basis, it may create the idea that their own needs and wants—which can be as simple as an hour on their own to read a book—are less important. However, if caregivers ignore their own needs, it can lead to a condition known as caregiver burnout, in which the person feels angry and resentful of the loved one they are helping. This may also lead to feelings of guilt because they do not want to resent their loved one who is in pain. Support groups can help prevent this in a number of ways. Groups for the person with chronic pain allow them to talk to someone besides their loved one about their pain, and support groups for caregivers allow them to talk to other people who understand what they are going through and can offer support and advice.

CHAPTER SIX

HOPE FOR THE FUTURE

While a life spent with chronic pain is not easy, there is reason to hope. From recent medical advances to the strength of the human spirit, there are many ways to combat and deal with chronic pain, and researchers are discovering more all the time.

Scientific Advances

Once seen as a symptom of another condition, pain is now recognized as a problem in and of itself. As a result, doctors and patients are better able to identify what might be causing pain and how it can be treated. There is a push to add pain to the list of vital signs, such as pulse and temperature, that are used to evaluate a patient's health, thanks to groups such as the American Pain Society, the American Pain Foundation, and the American Academy of Pain Medicine. In 2001, the Joint Commission on the Accreditation of Healthcare Organizations (JCAHO), which recognizes high-quality health care, announced a set of "pain standards" designed to improve the way facilities such as doctor's offices and hospitals diagnose and treat pain. Those who fail to meet these standards face losing their recognition.

Continuing research into the cause of chronic pain aims to make it easier to diagnose and treat pain-causing conditions. For instance, genetic researchers are examining the building blocks that make up the body to learn why some people process pain differently than others. They have identified that some pain sufferers do not have enough of a liver enzyme called CYP2D6, which plays a role in the painkilling process. By studying this enzyme further, scientists hope to develop treatments specifically for people who lack this enzyme. Other researchers are focused on a protein called "substance P," which seems to play a role in how the body senses and registers pain. Studies have shown that mice who lack this protein are better able to tolerate pain. Scientists hope that finding a way to block this protein might lead to new, more effective pain treatment options. In 2015, a study from Massachusetts General Hospital used brain scans to show that levels of an inflammation-linked protein are higher in areas that are known to influence pain transmission, which causes more glial activation. They hope this information will give them visible proof of people's pain. If it works, this would eliminate the need for patients to describe their pain on a scale; the doctor could simply measure the patient's protein levels to see how much pain they are in. However, more research is necessary to confirm these findings.

This ability to study pain on a genetic level is perhaps one of the most promising aspects of chronic pain research. Being able to see what makes each person's body work on a basic level could help scientists to one day develop personalized treatments designed for each patient. "We would love to be able to tell what, specifically, has gone wrong in each patient," said neurologist David Bennett of the University of Oxford. "Then we could say, 'Oh, you get this drug, whereas you get that other drug.'"[98] Given how far science has come in just the last few decades, such a future does not seem unreasonable. "[S]cientists … have made remarkable progress in understanding and treating pain in recent years," wrote Richard Laliberte, health journalist and former senior writer at *Men's Health*, so "doctors today have more options for dealing with discomfort than at any previous time in history."[99]

Continuing research has led to many advances in the diagnosis and treatment of chronic pain.

Some forms of chronic pain have seen more advancements than others. For example, for people with chronic back or leg pain, spinal cord stimulation (SCS) has frequently been used as a treatment. This involves placing electrodes on the body in precise spots to deliver electrical stimulation to the spine. Recently, researchers have tried a new form of SCS that uses much higher electrical stimulation for a shorter amount of time and have seen a long-term improvement in many patients. However, this treatment obviously would not work for people who have other types of chronic pain, which highlights the importance of continued research into all aspects of chronic pain disorders.

Technology versus Painkillers

Although strong painkillers such as opioids can effectively manage chronic pain, some people prefer not to take them. For some, it is because of the fear of becoming addicted; for others, they are allergic or do not like the way the drugs make them feel—for example, they may have trouble concentrating or even staying conscious. For these reasons, some companies are looking at ways technology can help people manage pain without opioids. In the past, it was not always easy to get companies to develop these devices because they were unsure of how much profit they would bring the company, but today a person can use Kickstarter or another crowdfunding website to make their product a reality.

One technological device that has recently become available is called Quell. It is a band that can be worn on a person's calf that gives off low-intensity electrical impulses to encourage the brain to produce more of its natural painkilling chemicals. Jennifer Kain Kilgore, a woman who has lived with chronic pain for years due to multiple car accidents, found that using Quell along with lower-dose painkillers helped her manage her pain and still keep her mental clarity, which was not the case when she tried opioids.

Other electrical impulse devices, such as the StimQ Peripheral Nerve Stimulator (PNS) can be implanted directly into the body near the site of the pain. Some people prefer this because they do not need to wear a large device all day; the StimQ, for instance, is powered by a small patch that can be worn on the clothes. However, since some chronic pain disorders do not have a specific pain site, these types of devices may not work for them. Although devices such as Quell and StimQ may not be 100 percent effective, they can provide immense relief for some types of chronic pain.

Many people are also using apps to help them manage their health. For example, the Triggr Health app can predict when a person who has struggled with opioid addiction in the past will relapse by analzying patterns in the way a person acts during a relapse. When it detects this danger, the app sets up a counseling appointment for the person with trained professionals who are available to chat through the app. Drug abuse counseling and other forms of therapy can be expensive, and some health insurance plans may not cover it; additionally, some people see a stigma around seeking help for drug abuse and would rather not let anyone know they have struggled with it. For these reasons, Triggr Health can be a huge benefit to someone who is dealing with an opioid addiction.

Changing Hearts and Minds

Progress has also been made in the way society views chronic pain and those who suffer from it. The IOM's 2011 report was made at the request of Congress and was the first of its kind to identify chronic pain as "America's largest invisible epidemic"[100] and recommend steps needed to advance pain treatment in the future. As advocacy groups and patients share their stories with others, they begin to break down the walls of judgment and misunderstanding that surround chronic pain and raise awareness. As Webster wrote,

Venom for Chronic Pain

Some treatments for chronic pain are still in the experimental stage and may sound bizarre or even a little frightening. One such treatment is the use of spider venom as a painkiller for people whose pain does not respond to current treatments. *Prevention* magazine explained,

> *Scientists recently identified seven compounds in tarantula venom that block an important step in your body's pain process. The paralytic essentially turns off one of the body's sodium channels, called Nav1.7, which sends pain signals to the brain ... But don't go scanning your pain reliever ingredients for spider venom. Scientists still need to figure out how to make it into a medicine that's safe for human use.[1]*

Similarly, researchers are looking at using bee venom the same way, mainly for people who suffer from arthritis:

> *[I]n one study, 82% of patients treated with bee venom acupuncture reported significant pain relief ... Honeybee venom increases blood circulation, softens tissues, reduces inflammation, and increases feel-good neurotransmitters like dopamine, norepinephrine, and serotonin, giving you an emotional boost in addition to treating your pain. Doctors sometimes prescribe sterilized bee venom for patients to inject themselves at home.[2]*

It is important to remember that chronic pain patients should discuss all treatments with their doctor before trying any themselves.

1. Kasandra Brabaw, "7 Totally Bizarre Treatments for Chronic Pain," *Prevention*, April 2, 2015. www.prevention.com/health/unusual-chronic-pain-treatments.

2. Brabaw, "7 Totally Bizarre Treatments for Chronic Pain."

I am old enough to remember when people with AIDS, mental illness, and cancer bore similar stigmas, and society has largely changed its attitudes in those cases. The same can happen with pain and pain treatment if we educate the public about what is really going on in the world of chronic pain.[101]

What Sets Chronic Pain Sufferers Apart

No matter what science or society thinks of chronic pain, those who live with it have a unique power to take control of their pain and how it affects their lives. The NIH has found that patients who are active in their pain treatment, such as getting involved in the decision-making process and making an effort to stay connected to loved ones, are better able to cope with their pain. Regardless of which treatments are currently available to them, chronic pain sufferers have a surprising amount of power when it comes to controlling how they view their pain—which can, in turn, influence how that pain affects them.

Chronic pain sufferers can learn to find happiness and joy in spite of their symptoms.

Gurnett has channeled his emotions into helping other people—which, he has found, has also helped him:

I didn't want anyone else to go through what I had gone through, and I viewed [starting a support group] as a way that I can give back something, even though I'm sick … It's given me a sense of purpose. It's something positive that I'm doing with my life, and I think that I'm setting a good example for some of the other chronically ill people my age, because it's very easy to give up. For other members, it appears that I've brought a small community together, and I've helped people who can't get out of the house much to be social, and I've helped people who have trouble making friends because they're sick make friends. And that is deeply satisfying.[102]

Chronic pain also has the ability to force patients to look at their lives differently. Living with pain and learning how to deal with it, physically and emotionally, can lead to a deeper appreciation for the positive things in life. Telaak, who finds comfort in her faith, said, "Every time I pray I say, 'Thank you, God, for today and every day.' Even when I am in pain, I know life is a gift, and I am so grateful. I also know that I will have good days, so those are the ones I focus on when I'm feeling poorly."[103]

Introduction:
What Makes Chronic Pain Different?

1. Institute of Medicine (IOM), *Relieving Pain in America: A Blueprint for Transforming Prevention, Care, Education, and Research.* Washington, DC: The National Academies Press, 2011, pp. 86–86.

2. David W. Swanson, ed., *Mayo Clinic on Chronic Pain.* Anstey, Leicester, UK: Ulverscroft Leicester, 2001, pp. 1–2.

3. Lynn R. Webster M.D., *The Painful Truth: What Chronic Pain Is Really Like and Why It Matters to Each of Us.* New York, NY: Oxford University Press, 2017, p. xviii.

Chapter One:
Understanding Chronic Pain

4. Melanie Thernstrom, *The Pain Chronicles: Cures, Myths, Mysteries, Prayers, Diaries, Brain Scans, Healing, and the Science of Suffering.* New York, NY: Farrar, Straus and Giroux, 2010, p. 43.

5. David B. Morris, *The Culture of Pain.* Berkeley, CA: University of California Press, 1991, p. 70.

6. Thernstrom, *The Pain Chronicles*, p. 87.

7. Quoted in Laurie Edwards, *In the Kingdom of the Sick: A Social History Of Chronic Illness In America.* New York, NY: Walker Publishing Company, Inc., 2013, p. 49.

8. Quoted in Swanson, *Mayo Clinic on Chronic Pain*, pp. 9–10.

9. Swanson, *Mayo Clinic on Chronic Pain*, p. 14.

10. Thernstrom, *The Pain Chronicles*, p. 139.

Chapter Two:
Chronic Pain Conditions

11. Swanson, *Mayo Clinic on Chronic Pain*, p. 30.

12. Edwards, *In the Kingdom of the Sick*, p. 110.

13. Cait Telaak, e-mail interview by author, August 14, 2017.

Chapter Three:
The Effects of Chronic Pain

14. Webster, *The Painful Truth*, p. 13.

15. Kristen Spinola, "6 Challenges Healthy People May Not Realize Are Caused by Chronic Pain," The Mighty, May 13, 2016. themighty. com/2016/05/side-effects-of-chronic-pain/.

16. Spinola, "6 Challenges Healthy People May Not Realize Are Caused by Chronic Pain."

17. Swanson, *Mayo Clinic on Chronic Pain*, pp. 59-61.

18. Webster, *The Painful Truth*, p. 55.

19. Quoted in Edwards, *In the Kingdom of the Sick*, p. 103.

20. Kristen Spinola, "The Unpredictability of Life with Chronic Pain," The Mighty, May 10, 2016. themighty.com/2016/05/dealing-with-unpredictable-life-with-chronic-pain/.

21. Quoted in Rachel Noble Benner, "Chronic Pain Not Only Hurts, It also Causes Isolation and Depression. But There's Hope," *Washington Post*, January 12, 2015. www.washingtonpost. com/national/health-science/chronic-pain-not-only-hurts-it-also-causes-isolation-and-

depression-but-theres-hope/2015/01/12/
db576178-7fe7-11e4-81fd-8c4814dfa9d7_
story.html?utm_term=.752b8aaa12dd.

22. Thernstrom, *The Pain Chronicles*, p. 186.

23. Ryan Gurnett, interview by author, August 14, 2017.

24. Richard Laliberte, *Doctors' Guide to Chronic Pain: The Newest, Quickest, and Most Effective Ways to Find Relief.* Pleasantville, NY: The Reader's Digest Association, Inc., 2003, p. 132.

25. Christy Kassler, e-mail interview by author, August 8, 2017.

26. Telaak, interview.

27. Edwards, *In the Kingdom of the Sick*, pp. 109–110.

28. Noble Benner, "Chronic Pain."

29. Telaak, interview.

30. Crystal Fudalik, e-mail interview by author, August 18, 2017.

31. Lauren Brooke, "When People Judge Me for Not Working Because of My Chronic Pain," The Mighty, December 30, 2016. themighty. com/2016/12/chronic-pain-judge-me-for-not-working/.

32. Telaak, interview.

33. Webster, *The Painful Truth*, pp. 208, 214.

34. Webster, *The Painful Truth*, pp. 213–214.

35. Gurnett, interview.

36. Quoted in Edwards, *In the Kingdom of the Sick*, p. 55.

37. Webster, *The Painful Truth*, p. 5.

38. IOM, *Relieving Pain in America*, pp. 1,109.

39. IOM, *Relieving Pain in America*, pp. 86–87.

40. IOM, *Relieving Pain in America*, p. 93.

41. IOM, *Relieving Pain in America*, pp. 92–93.

Chapter Four:
Treating Chronic Pain

42. Claire Suddath, "Living with Pain," *TIME*, March 11, 2011. content. time.com/time/specials/packages/article/0,28804,2053382_2055269_2055261-4,00. html.

43. IOM, *Relieving Pain in America*, p. 144.

44. Laliberte, *Doctors' Guide to Chronic Pain*, p. 86.

45. Edwards, *In the Kingdom of the Sick*, p. 171.

46. Laliberte, *Doctors' Guide to Chronic Pain*, p. 17.

47. Swanson, *Mayo Clinic on Chronic Pain*, pp. 230–231.

48. Fudalik, interview.

49. Swanson, *Mayo Clinic on Chronic Pain*, p. 227.

50. Gurnett, interview.

51. Quoted in Laliberte, *Doctors' Guide to Chronic Pain*, p. 41.

52. IOM, *Relieving Pain in America*, p. 126.

53. Laliberte, *Doctors' Guide to Chronic Pain*, p. 17.

54. Laliberte, *Doctors' Guide to Chronic Pain*, p. 27.

55. Fudalik, interview.

56. Laliberte, *Doctors' Guide to Chronic Pain*, p. 82.

57. Laliberte, *Doctors' Guide to Chronic Pain*, p. 82.

58. Laliberte, *Doctors' Guide to Chronic Pain*, p. 72.

59. Kassler, interview.

60. Swanson, *Mayo Clinic on Chronic Pain*, p. 71.

61. Fudalik, interview.

62. Swanson, *Mayo Clinic on Chronic Pain*, p. 137.

Chapter Five:
The Trouble With "Invisible Illnesses"

63. Fudalik, interview.

64. Quoted in Edwards, *In the Kingdom of the Sick*, p. 53.

65. Telaak, interview.

66. Telaak, interview.

67. Sean Bishop, interview by author, August 14, 2017.

68. Telaak, interview.

69. Fudalik, interview.

70. Quoted in Edwards, *In the Kingdom of the Sick*, p. 27.

71. IOM, *Relieving Pain in America*, p. 152.

72. Swanson, *Mayo Clinic on Chronic Pain*, p. 74.

73. Edwards, *In the Kingdom of the Sick*, p. 33.

74. Morris, *The Culture of Pain*, pp. 70-71.

75. Telaak, interview.

76. Fudalik, interview.

77. Kate Eastman, "When You're Too Scared to Use Your Disability Parking Permit," The Mighty, November 12, 2015. themighty. com/2015/11/being-too-scared-to-use-your-disability-parking-permit/.

78. Tressia Demaskie, "I Don't Owe You an Explanation When I Do Something Fun Despite My Chronic Pain," The Mighty, December 8, 2016. themighty.com/2016/12/judgment-having-fun-chronic-pain/.

79. Telaak, interview.

80. Lisa Prins, "The Exhaustion of Fighting With Doctors for a Diagnosis," The Mighty, June 1, 2017. themighty.com/2017/06/chronic-illness-fighting-with-doctors-for-diagnosis/.

81. Swanson, *Mayo Clinic on Chronic Pain*, "About Chronic Pain."

82. Laliberte, *Doctors' Guide to Chronic Pain*, p. 11.

83. IOM, *Relieving Pain in America*, pp. 119–120.

84. Quoted in Laliberte, *Doctors' Guide to Chronic Pain*, p. 152.

85. Telaak, interview.

86. Laliberte, *Doctors' Guide to Chronic Pain*, p. 155.

87. Edwards, *In the Kingdom of the Sick*, p. 115.

88. Edwards, *In the Kingdom of the Sick*, p. 116.

89. "Women Experience More Chronic Pain Than Men—Now We Know Why," The Conversation, October 30, 2013. theconversation.com/women-experience-more-chronic-pain-than-men-now-we-know-why-19648.

90. "Women Experience More Chronic Pain Than Men," The Conversation.

91. Quoted in Webster, *The Painful Truth*, p. 173.

92. Gurnett, interview.

93. "Testimonial Paula," YouTube video, 1:08, posted by TMJAssociation, June 2, 2015. youtu.be/2zDrhvrG6Ds.

94. Gurnett, interview.

95. Quoted in Edwards, *In the Kingdom of the Sick*, p. 120.

96. Telaak, interview.

97. Lee Woodruff, "Caring for a Loved One with Chronic Pain: The Four Caregiver Cornerstones," *Huffington Post*, last updated November 17, 2011. www.huffingtonpost.com/lee-woodruff/caring-for-a-loved-one-wi_b_846186.html.

Chapter Six:
Hope for the Future

98. Stephani Sutherland, "Pain That Won't Quit," *Scientific American*, vol. 311, no. 6, Dec. 2014, p. 67.

99. Laliberte, *Doctors' Guide to Chronic Pain*, p. 164.

100. Webster, *The Painful Truth*, p. 209.

101. Webster, *The Painful Truth*, p. 215.

102. Gurnett, interview.

103. Telaak, interview.

anesthetic: A drug or other substance that makes a patient unable to feel sensations such as pain, either throughout the body (general anesthesia) or in a particular location (local anesthesia), so surgery or another painful procedure can be performed.

anxiety: A mental disorder in which patients experience an increased state of worry and uneasiness.

circulation: The movement of blood through the heart and veins, which carries oxygen and nutrients to and removes waste products from various parts of the body.

cognitive: Of or related to mental processes such as judgment, memory, perception, and reasoning.

depression: A mental disorder in which patients experience symptoms such as sadness, loss of hope, and numbness.

digestive: Of or related to digestion, which is the breaking down of food into nutrients and other substances so they can be absorbed by the body.

enzyme: A protein found in the cells that helps with natural processes in the body, such as digestion.

immune system: The body system that protects the body from and fights off viruses, infection, and disease.

inflammation: Redness, swelling, pain, tenderness, and heat caused by tissue damage.

narcotics: A category of strong drugs that can cause numbness to pain and other sensations.

opioid: A kind of narcotic produced from the opium plant.

self-advocacy: The practice of patients speaking for themselves, actively participating in their treatment, and looking out for their own interests rather than depending on others to do this for them.

American Academy of Pain Medicine
8735 W. Higgins Rd., Suite 300
Chicago, IL 60631
(847) 375-4731
www.painmed.org
This organization is the medical society that represents physicians practicing in the field of pain medicine. See the "Patient Center" section of its website for information on pain management and to locate physicians by area.

American Chronic Pain Association
P.O. Box 850
Rocklin, CA 95677
(800) 533-3231
theacpa.org
The American Chronic Pain Association offers peer support and education in pain management skills to people with pain, their family and friends, and health care professionals.

American Herbal Products Association
8630 Fenton St., Suite 918
Silver Spring, MD 20910
(301) 588-1171
www.ahpa.org
The American Herbal Products Association is a trade organization that represents the manufacturers of dietary supplements and acts as an advocate for the industry during Congressional hearings and similar forums. Visitors to the organization's website can find press releases and answers to frequently asked questions about herbal supplements for conditions such as chronic pain.

Mayo Clinic
13400 E. Shea Blvd.
Scottsdale, AZ 85259
(480) 301-8000
www.mayoclinic.org
This not-for-profit organization is dedicated to clinical practice, education, and research and to providing expert, whole-person care to patients with a wide variety of health issues. See the "Patient Care and Health Information" section of the website for information on specific conditions, including symptoms and treatments.

Narcotics Anonymous
P.O. Box 9999
Van Nuys, CA 91409
(818) 773-9999
www.na.org
Narcotics Anonymous is a nonprofit organization that helps people recover from addiction to narcotics. Members support each other in their recovery by sharing their experiences in group meetings. A list of meeting locations can be found on the website.

National Fibromyalgia & Chronic Pain Association
31 Federal Ave.
Logan, UT 84321
(801) 200-3627
www.fmcpaware.org
This organization unites patients; policy makers; and health care, medical, and scientific communities to transform lives through visionary support, advocacy, research, and education of fibromyalgia and chronic pain illnesses.

Books

Berne, Katrina, Ph.D. *Chronic Fatigue Syndrome, Fibromyalgia and Other Invisible Illnesses: The Comprehensive Guide.* 3rd ed. Alameda, CA: Hunter House, 2002.
This book is a guide to several common invisible illnesses, as well as an exploration of what invisible illness does to patients' lives and how patients can help themselves.

Bula, Ania. *Young, Sick, and Invisible: A Skeptic's Journey with Chronic Illness.* Durham, NC: Pitchstone Publishing, 2016.
This is an honest and humorous account of one chronic pain sufferer's real-life experiences as a young adult with a hard-to-understand condition.

Natelson, Benjamin H., M.D. *Your Symptoms Are Real: What to Do When Your Doctor Says Nothing Is Wrong.* Hoboken, NJ: John Wiley & Sons, Inc., 2008.
Written by a doctor, this guide teaches patients with invisible illnesses how they can take control of their treatment and practice self-advocacy.

Rosenfeld, Arthur. *The Truth About Chronic Pain: Patients and Professionals on How to Face It, Understand It, Overcome It.* New York, NY: Basic Books, 2003.
Patients describe, in their own words, what it is like to live with chronic pain and the ways society, including health care professionals, fails to meet their needs.

Selak, Joy H., and Steven S. Overman, M.D. *You Don't Look Sick! Living Well With Invisible Chronic Illness.* 2nd ed. New York, NY: Demos Health, 2013.
This book is a chronicle of one patient's journey of chronic invisible illness—from diagnosis to acceptance and coping.

Websites

But You Don't Look Sick
www.butyoudontlooksick.com
Run by the woman who created the Spoon Theory, this website offers information, networking, support, and community for those living with chronic and invisible illnesses.

ChronicBabe
www.chronicbabe.com
This website is a motivational online community for young women with chronic health issues, including chronic pain and other invisible illnesses.

The Mighty
www.themighty.com
This blog publishes posts by real people who live with disability, disease, and mental illness. See the "Conditions A-Z" section for posts on particular topics, including chronic pain and specific conditions.

The Pain Community
www.paincommunity.org
This organization offers a blog, community, and education and advocacy resources for those affected by pain.

Spine-health: Chronic Pain Health Center
www.spine-health.com/conditions/chronic-pain
This independent website offers medically reviewed tips on how to deal with chronic pain, with a focus on pain in the neck and back.

A

B

C

G

Gabapentin, 44
Gaga: Five Foot Two, 46
Gallup poll, 28
genetics, 16, 20, 78–79
glia, 73, 79
grieving process, 34
guilt, 30–31, 34, 77
Gurnett, Ryan, 31, 38, 54, 74–75, 83

H

headaches, 19–21, 23–24, 51, 54
health insurance, 37, 81
heat and cold therapy, 47
herniated disc, 21
humor therapy, 57
hydrocodone, 44
hypnosis, 52–53

I

injections, 46
injury, 6, 8–9, 11, 13–17, 19, 21, 25
Institute of Medicine (IOM), 7, 16, 41, 45, 55, 67, 70
irritable bowel syndrome (IBS), 24, 59

J

jobs, 34
Johns Hopkins, 29, 33
Joint Commission on the Accreditation of Healthcare
    Organizations (JCAHO), 78
Journal of the American Medical Association, The (JAMA), 69

K

Kassler, Christy, 32, 58

L

Lady Gaga, 46
Lamictal, 44
"life cycle" categories, 16
lifestyle changes, 31, 59–60
loneliness, 28–29, 33, 35
Lortab, 44

Kelly Gurnett is a freelance writer and editor whose work has appeared on websites such as *The Penny Hoarder, Huffington Post,* and *Business Insider.* Kelly's husband Ryan has been diagnosed with mitochondrial myopathy, and Kelly has been diagnosed with migraines. She lives in Buffalo, NY, where she earned a B.A. in English and Religious Studies from Canisius College. She attends an invisible illness game night/support group for young adults, run by her husband, twice a month.